One Hundred Countries,
Two Billion People

One Hundred Countries, Two Billion People

THE DIMENSIONS OF DEVELOPMENT

Robert S. McNamara

PRAEGER PUBLISHERS
New York • Washington • London

PRAEGER PUBLISHERS
111 Fourth Avenue, New York, N.Y. 10003, U.S.A.
5, Cromwell Place, London SW7 2JL, England

Published in the United States of America in 1973
by Praeger Publishers, Inc.

© 1973 by Praeger Publishers, Inc.

Library of Congress Cataloging in Publication Data
McNamara, Robert S   1916-
  One hundred countries, two billion people.
  Includes bibliographical references.
  1. Underdeveloped areas. 2. Economic development. 3. International
Bank for Reconstruction and Development. I. Title.
HC59.7.M22   338.91   73-756

Contents

Preface

In the five years I have been President of the World Bank
I have continually been impressed with the need for political
leaders and the public to reflect more deeply on the problems
faced by the two billion people, hundreds of millions of
whom are literally struggling for survival, in the one hundred
developing nations that we serve. Admittedly, that kind of
reflection is not easy. For one thing, the development process
itself is extraordinarily complex. For another, the pressures of
day-to-day events, month-to-month crises, and year-to-year
political preoccupations tend to distract the attention of even
the well-informed from the more profound problems of the
world.

Nevertheless, the underlying drive toward social and economic transformation in the developing world is a critical

component of the central historical movement of our time. The character of international life in the next century—for rich and poor nations alike—will depend largely on the success of the development effort.

Still another obstacle to thinking about development in a realistic manner is that traditional measures of progress are usually expressed in over-all economic statistics. As useful, and even necessary, as these gross statistics are, they sometimes obscure the essence of the problem. Development is about people. The only criterion for measuring its ultimate success or failure is what it does to enhance the lives of individual human beings.

Most of the developing countries are making progress in over-all statistical terms. But hundreds of millions of people living in those countries are caught up in conditions of deprivation that no set of statistics can begin to describe. The truth is that poverty in the developing world is an intolerable assault on human dignity and decency. Malnutrition, disease, illiteracy, unemployment, and early death pervade these vast populations.

If development cannot alter that situation, development will have failed.

But development can and will alter it, can and will help create the conditions in which those hundreds of millions of human beings will have the opportunity more fully to realize the potential inherent in their lives—provided all of us take the necessary steps.

That is what the entire development community—international and national, official and private—has as its task. But public discussion and debate of these issues are critical to the success of the whole development process. If development is to succeed in any acceptable time frame, it demands strong political leadership, backed by informed and articulate public support.

With a view to encouraging such discussion, I have gathered here in one volume my principal public statements on development made in the course of the past five years. Their general line of argument encompasses seven major themes:

• The discouragement over development that appeared in certain quarters of the affluent world in the late 1960's was based on two erroneous assumptions: that the wealthy countries could no longer afford to supply assistance to the poor nations in adequate amounts; and that, even if these affluent countries could afford it, it would be unwise, since the record of development aid was characterized by waste, incompetence, and failure. Both those suppositions were untrue, but they weakened the aid effort. In 1968 we in the World Bank* introduced a Five-Year Program of greatly expanded assistance to our developing member countries in order to counter this trend and to set in motion shifts in strategy to meet the evolving character of development itself.

• Essential to any reassessment of the needs of development is the recognition that the population problem must be faced up to squarely and seen for what it in fact is—the greatest single obstacle to the economic and social advancement of the majority of the peoples in the developing world. Admittedly complex and sensitive, the problem is compounded by a series of myths and misunderstandings that stand in the way

* The World Bank, a specialized agency of the United Nations, founded at the Bretton Woods Monetary and Financial Conference in 1944, now consists of the International Bank for Reconstruction and Development (IBRD), the International Development Association (IDA), and the International Finance Corporation (IFC). The IBRD's principal role is to make loans to developing countries for a wide variety of productive projects. The IDA performs the same functions as the IBRD and has the same organization, management, and staff, but its loans are on highly concessionary terms and are made to the poorest nations. The IFC was established to assist in promoting the international flow of private capital to the developing countries and to participate in the financing of private enterprise in those countries. Unless otherwise indicated in the text, the terms "World Bank" and "Bank" apply to all these institutions.

of any rational and humane solution. The first step toward dealing with these misunderstandings is to recognize the costly dangers of delay in taking appropriate action.

• Excessive rates of population growth are contributing today to severe malnutrition, and to chronic urban and rural unemployment. To bring population growth into reasonable equilibrium with economic growth will require decades of effort. It is imperative in the meantime that we fashion new strategies to combat directly the malnutrition and unemployment that will otherwise inevitably occur.

• Economic advance in the developing countries does require foreign exchange—far more than is currently being made available. The modest goal of the United Nations Second Development Decade for concessionary aid was that the affluent countries should, by 1975, increase their aid to .7 per cent of their combined gross national products. It now seems clear that only half that goal will be achieved. The result will be that the poorest countries—those with the greatest need—will suffer the most. With so massive a shortfall in aid, it becomes all the more imperative that the affluent nations dismantle the discriminatory barriers to trade that prevent the poor nations from increasing their exports. The developing nations must be given a fair chance to earn the foreign exchange necessary to manage their mounting debt burdens and to finance their agricultural and industrial expansion.

• Increased trade by itself, however, will not be enough. Action to increase aid—and thereby to reduce the shortfall—must also be taken. To do so, the rich nations are not being asked to diminish their present riches. They are only being asked to share a tiny percentage of their continually increasing wealth. The fundamental question they must ask themselves is this: Which is ultimately more in their national interest—to funnel the total future increment in national income into an endlessly spiraling consumer economy (with all its by-products of waste and pollution) or to dedicate a modest share of that increment to improving the fundamental quality of life in the developing world?

• If economic growth accelerates in the poorer countries, the environmental problem will deserve serious consideration. But our experience in the World Bank is that the problem is manageable. There is no evidence that the development the poor nations so desperately require will place an unacceptable burden either on their own or on anybody else's environment.

• Finally, it is becoming increasingly clear that the critical issue within the developing economies is not simply the rate of growth but the *nature* of growth. In these countries' pursuit of rapid economic advance, the poorest 40 per cent of their populations are being largely left behind. The task, then, for these governments is to reorient their development policies in order to attack directly the personal poverty of this huge and most deprived segment of their people. This the governments can do without abandoning their goals of vigorous over-all economic growth. But they must be prepared to give greater priority to establishing growth targets in terms of essential human needs—in terms of nutrition, housing, health, literacy, and employment—even if it be at the cost of some reduction in the pace of advance in certain narrow and highly privileged sectors whose benefits accrue only to the few.

These, then, are the principal themes I have explored in my public statements on development policy. What follow in this volume are the statements themselves, edited only for clarity and cohesion. The careful reader will note considerable reiteration of some of the basic themes—notably the adverse effects on development of high rates of population growth, and both the necessity for and the capability of the developed nations to increase the level of their assistance to the developing nations. Statistics have been updated where useful or necessary. No effort, however, has been made to alter the line of argument with the benefit of hindsight.*

While the statements represent my personal views, I am indebted to the staff of the Bank and to many friends and scholars (particularly Miss Barbara Ward, Dr. Bernard Berelson, and the participants, from both developing and developed nations, of the Bellagio Conferences, organized by the Ford and Rockefeller foundations) whose reflections on these issues have enriched my own thinking. I should add a special word of appreciation to my senior colleagues in the Bank who have read and commented on the drafts of all my public statements, and to Mr. Jack Maddux who has contributed so much to their preparation.

It is to these men and women—and indeed to all those whose goal is to assist the two billion people of the developing world to achieve a level of life more in accord with fundamental human dignity—that I dedicate this volume as I enter my second term as President of the World Bank.

Robert S. McNamara

April, 1973

* Occasions, places, and times of delivery are listed under "Sources" at the end of the book.

One Hundred Countries, Two Billion People

1

The Task of Development

I have always regarded the World Bank as something more than a Bank—as a development agency—and when I came to it as President, I was not entirely a stranger to the problems of world development. As United States Secretary of Defense I had observed and spoken publicly about the connection between world poverty and unstable relations among nations.* Yet I was uneasily aware that the peoples of the world, as they looked at the 1960's, felt a deep sense of frustration and failure. The rich countries felt that they had given billions of dollars without achieving much in the way of development; the poor countries felt that too little of the enormous increases in the wealth of the developed world had been

* See, for example, a speech delivered at a meeting of the American Association of Newspaper Editors in 1966, reprinted in *The Essence of Security*, by Robert S. McNamara (New York: Harper and Row, 1968).

diverted to help them rise out of the pit of poverty in which they had been engulfed for centuries past.

There have been successes. Many billions in aid have been forthcoming from the developed world, and as a result of that aid and of the increased capacity of the poorer countries to manage their affairs, their economic growth has been stimulated.

Aid does work. It is not money wasted; it is a sound investment. Even the goal of the First Development Decade—an annual rise in national incomes in the poorer countries of 5 per cent by 1970—was finally achieved. That was an unprecedented rate of growth.

Yet we all know that these cheerful statistics are cosmetics that conceal a far less cheerful picture in many countries. The oil-rich nations of the Middle East have prospered economically; so have some small states in East Asia. But, for the nations of Africa and South Asia—nations with a total population of over 1 billion—the average increase in national income is, at most, 3.9 per cent and much of the growth is concentrated in the industrial areas, while the peasant remains stuck in his immemorial poverty, living on the bare margin of subsistence.

Casting its shadow over this scene is the mushrooming cloud of the population explosion. If we take this into account, and look at the progress of human beings rather than of nations, the growth figures appear even less acceptable.

The annual growth of per capita income in Latin America is about 2 per cent, in East Asia about 3 per cent, in Africa 2.5 per cent, and in South Asia only about 1.3 per cent. At these rates, a doubling of per capita income in East Asia would take nearly twenty-four years, in Latin America more than thirty-five years, in Africa almost twenty-nine years, and in South Asia more than half a century. Even in the most progressive of these areas, the amount of improvement would be imperceptible to the average citizen from year to year.

Such a situation cries out for a greater and more urgent effort by the richer nations to assist economic growth in these poorer countries. The richer nations are financially capable of such action. During the First Development Decade, they added more than $700 billion to their annual real incomes, a sum far greater than the total annual incomes of the under-developed countries of Asia, Africa, and Latin America. But while the requirement for assistance was never higher, the will to provide it was never lower in many, though not all, of the countries that provide the bulk of economic aid.

The disenchantment of the rich with the future of development aid was fed by performance deficiencies of many of the poorer nations. Blatant mismanagement of economies, diversion of scarce resources to wars of nationalism, and the perpetuation of discriminatory systems of social organization and income distribution have been all too common in these countries.

When I came to the World Bank in 1968, I found this confused but sharply disappointing picture of the development world. It was difficult to see what had gone wrong in the past, although something clearly had, or what was the right path to follow in the future.

In these circumstances, I turned to a suggestion put forward by my predecessor, Mr. George Woods. This was that we should establish a commission of men well versed in world affairs and accustomed to influencing them, who would survey the past aid effort, seek out its lessons for the future, and then examine that future to see what needs to be done by the nations of the world—rich and poor, developed and underdeveloped alike—to promote the economic well-being of the great majority of mankind. At my request, Mr. Lester

B. Pearson, formerly Prime Minister of Canada, agreed to direct such a survey and served as Chairman of the Commission on International Development, which proceeded completely independently of the Bank and produced its report in October, 1969.* The Pearson Commission turned our eyes to the long future, pointing out guidelines not just for the next decade but for a whole generation of development that would carry us to the end of the century.

But in 1968 there was much for us to do immediately. It was apparent that even after a decade dedicated to development the income gap between the developed and the developing countries had increased, was increasing, and ought to be diminished. But it was equally clear that the political will to foster development had weakened further and needed desperately to be strengthened.

What could the World Bank do in this situation? I was determined that it would act—that it would not share in the general paralysis which was afflicting aid efforts in so many parts of the world. I did not believe that the Bank by itself could do the job of development that needed to be done throughout the world, but I did believe that it could provide the leadership and could show that it was not resources that were lacking (the richer countries had resources in plenty) but the will to employ those resources in the development of the poorer nations.

We in the Bank, therefore, set out to survey the next five years. We formulated a "development plan" for each developing nation, to see what the World Bank could invest if there were no shortage of funds and if the only limit on our activities were the capacity of our member countries to use our

* Other Commissioners were: Sir Edward Boyle, United Kingdom; Roberto de Oliveira Campos, Brazil; C. Douglas Dillon, United States; Wilfried Guth, West Germany; Sir Arthur Lewis, Jamaica; Robert E. Marjolin, France; and Saburo Okita, Japan. Their report was entitled *Partners in Development* (New York: Praeger, 1969).

assistance effectively and to repay our loans on the terms on which they were lent. As a result of this survey, we concluded that a very substantial increase in World Bank activities was desirable and possible.

In addressing the Bank's Board of Governors (broadly an assembly of the world's Finance Ministers) in September, 1968, I felt it prudent and fitting to present to them an outline of my thinking on this crucial decision. Now, more than four years later, I see no reason to alter the words I used at the time:

Let me begin by defining some orders of magnitude: I believe that globally the World Bank should during the next five years lend twice as much as during the past five years. This means that between 1968 and 1973 the Bank would lend in total nearly as much as it has lent since it began operations nearly twenty-three years ago.

This is a change of such a degree that I feel it necessary to emphasize that it is not a change of kind. We believe that we can carry out these operations within the high standards of careful evaluation and sound financing that my predecessors have made synonymous with the name of the World Bank.

Our loans will be for projects as soundly based and appraised as any in our history. However, more and more, in looking for projects to support, we shall look for those that contribute most fundamentally to the development of the total national economy, seeking to break strangle holds on development and to find growth opportunities that stimulate further growth. And our help will be directed to those poor nations that need it most.

This I believe to be sound development financing, but it is not riskproof, and I do not believe that the utter avoidance of risks is the path of prudence or wisdom. For instance, I recently visited Indonesia, where, for good reasons, the Bank has never made a loan of any sort in the past. What I found was the sixth largest nation in the world, rich in natural resources, striving in the wake of the most terrible disasters, both economic and political, to set itself straight on the path to development. Without external help Indonesia faces certain disaster; by giving help (as we have begun to do through the International Development Association and through the establishment of a permanent mission), we are running some risks. I do not believe anyone would wish it otherwise.

The parable of the talents is a parable about power—about financial power—and it illuminates the great truth that all power is given us to be used, not to be wrapped in a napkin against risk.

But if we are to lend at double the level of the past, can we raise the money? I will not speak now about the soft-loan money, which is raised by government contributions—we all know how essential these funds are—but about the money we raise by bond issues in the capital markets of the world. I am confident that the money is there, because I have confidence in the immense capacity of the economies of the developed world. No country need fear bankrupting itself because it plays its full part in development.

There are, of course, certain constraints resulting from balance of payments difficulties, but I am fully aware that the balance of payments difficulty is a problem of balance among the rich economies and not of balance between those countries as a group and the rest of the world. Very little of the money lent in aid stays in the developing countries. Almost all of it returns quickly in payment for the goods purchased in the richer countries. It is our job in the World Bank to look at the world money markets as a whole and see where there are surpluses and reserves that can be tapped. Following this line, we have gone to the Middle East and successfully raised funds there, as well as in the more conventional markets of the world—in particular, the Federal Republic of Germany and the United States. As a result, within ninety days in 1968, the World Bank raised more funds by borrowing than in the whole of any single calendar year in its history.*

I would stress that in doubling the World Bank lending activities, we shall not depart from our high standards of investment policy. On the other hand, it should not be thought that our policy is simply "more of the same." Our five-year prospect calls for considerable change in the allocation of our resources, both to geographical areas and to economic sectors.

First as to area: In the past the World Bank has tended to concentrate its effort on the South Asian subcontinent. Much has been achieved—the harnessing of the waters of the Indus River system for power and irrigation, for instance—and much remains to be achieved. I believe World Bank lending to Asia should increase substantially over the next five years. But it is not to Asia alone that our new effort will be directed. It is to Latin America and Africa as well, where our past activities have been less concentrated, and to countries in great need of our help, such as Indonesia and the United Arab Republic, where our past activities have been negligible.

In Latin America, I foresee our investment rate more than doubling in the next five years. But it is in Africa, just coming to the threshold of major investment for development, that the greatest expansion of our activities should take place. There, with effective collaboration from the African countries during the next five years, we should increase our rate of investment threefold.

Further changes will flow from our shift to a greater em-

* An account of the Bank's borrowing in 1968–73 is given in the Appendix.

phasis on Africa and Latin America. The states of these two continents are smaller than the giant states of Asia. There will be many more projects, but they will be smaller and will demand much more staff work per million dollars lent than in the past.

The work of the Bank will also be increased because in many of the countries in which we will now be investing there is no well-established development plan or planning organization. We shall try, in conjunction with other sources of funds, to help these countries to develop plans and to adopt wise and appropriate policies for development—in some cases by establishing resident missions as we have done in Indonesia—but always remembering that it is their country, their economy, their culture, and their aspirations that we seek to assist.

In particular, we will exert special efforts to right one upside-down aspect of our operations: Many of our poorest members, despite their greater need, have had the least technical and financial assistance from the World Bank. About ten of these have had no loans or credits at all, largely because of their inability to prepare projects for consideration. In these cases we will provide special assistance to improve economic performance and to identify and prepare projects acceptable for our financing.

With the doubling of World Bank lending and with the increase in the complexity of our operations, there will clearly be a need for an increase in professional staff, as well as for some streamlining of procedures. We are now engaged in a worldwide recruiting drive to find people with the high standards of expertise and dedication that have always been the attributes of the staff. I am anxious that this should really be an international bank, in fact as well as in name, and I intend to ensure that we move steadily in the direction of the widest possible distribution in the nationalities of our staff.*

Not only should our lending double in volume and shift geographically, but we can foresee, as well, dramatic changes among sectors of investment. Great increases will occur in the sectors of education and agriculture. My predecessor, as President of the World Bank, George Woods, began to place increased emphasis on education, a relatively new field for the Bank. In recent years the Bank has been seeking, hesitantly but with a growing sense of urgency, to find its optimum role in this field.

We are aware of the immense numbers of illiterates in the developing world: about 30 per cent in Latin America, 60 per cent in Asia, 80 per cent in tropical Africa. We know too that education is relevant to all aspects of development. It makes a more effective worker, a more creative manager, a better farmer, a more efficient administrator, a human being closer to self-fulfillment.

The need is clear, but it has been less clear how the Bank's resources can be brought to bear on this labyrinthine problem. Now, after some years of collaboration with Unesco, we believe we have found a way of increasing Bank investment in education—investment that we hope will call forth further investment by the governments of the developing countries themselves.

Our aim here will be to provide assistance where it will contribute most to economic development. This will mean emphasis on educational planning, the starting point for the whole process of educational improvement. It will mean assistance, particularly in teacher training, at all levels, from primary to university. It will mean expansion of our support for a variety of other educational activities, including the

* In 1972, staff members of the World Bank represented more than one hundred nationalities.

training of managers, entrepreneurs, and, of course, agriculturists.

It is important to emphasize that education, normally one of the largest employers in any country, is one of the few industries that has not undergone a technological revolution. We must help to move it out of the handicraft stage. With the terrible and growing shortage of qualified teachers all over the developing world, we must find ways to make good teachers more productive. This will involve investment in textbooks, in audio-visual materials, and above all in the use of modern communications techniques (radio, film, and television) for teaching purposes.

To carry out this program we would hope over the next five years to increase our lending for educational development at least threefold.

But the sector of greatest expansion in our Five-Year Program is agriculture, which has for so long been the stepchild of development. Here again there has never been any doubt about its importance. About two-thirds of the people of the developing world live on the soil, yet these countries have to import annually $4 billion of food from the industrialized nations. Even then their diet is so indaquate, in many cases, that they cannot do an effective day's work and, more ominous still, there is growing scientific evidence that the dietary deficiencies of the parent are passed on as mental deficiencies to the children.

The need has stared us in the face for decades past. But how to help?

In the past, investment in agricultural improvement produced but a modest yield; the traditional seeds and plants did better with irrigation and fertilizer, but the increase in yield was not dramatic. In the past twenty years, however, research has resulted in a break-through in the production of new strains of wheat and rice and other plants that can improve yields by three to five times. What is more, these new strains are particularly sensitive to the input of water and fertilizer. Badly managed, they will produce little more than traditional yields, but with correct management they will give the peasant an unprecedented crop.

Here is an opportunity for irrigation, fertilizer, and peasant education to produce near miracles. The farmer himself in one short season can see the beneficial results of that scientific agriculture that has seemed so often in the past to be a will-o'-the-wisp, tempting him to innovation without benefit.

Our task now is to enable the peasant to make the most of this opportunity. With the continuing assistance of the Food and Agriculture Organization, we intend to do so at once and in good measure. Irrigation schemes, fertilizer plants, agricultural research and extension, the production of pesticides, agricultural machinery, storage facilities—with all of these we will press ahead in the immediate future. In 1969, we plan to process more than twice the value of agricultural loans than in the past, and our agricultural dollar loan volume over the next five years should quadruple.

There is an element of risk in all this, of course. Seeds for the new strains of plants were issued before all the tests had been completed. The resistance of the crops to local diseases or pests cannot yet be ensured, and the splendid harvests in India and Pakistan this year [1968] cannot all be attributed to the new seeds. But I have no doubt, though setbacks may lie ahead, that we are now on the brink of an agricultural revolution as significant as any development since the Industrial Revolution. It is one that gives us a breathing spell in the race between man and his resources.

This leads me to yet another area where the Bank needs to take new initiatives—the control of population growth. This is a thorny subject that would be very much more conveniently left alone. But I cannot do so, because the World

Bank is concerned above all with economic development, and the rapid growth of population is one of the greatest barriers to the economic growth and social well-being of our member states.

This is the aspect of the population problem with which I shall deal, because it is this aspect which most closely concerns the World Bank and its members. It makes it impossible for any of us to brush the subject aside, however strong our inclinations to do so may be.

The terrifying statistics of population growth as a whole can best be appreciated in the context of a long perspective. Some 2 million years were required for the population of the world to reach 3 billion. At current growth rates only 35 years will be required to add another 3 billion.

As a development planner, I wish to deal only with the hard facts of population impact on economic growth. Recent studies show the crippling effect of a high rate of population increase on economic growth in any developing country. For example, take two typical developing countries with similar standards of living, each with a birth rate of 40 per thousand (the actual rate in India and Mexico), and estimate what would happen if the birth rate in one of those countries, in a period of twenty-five years, were to be halved to 20 per thousand, a rate still well above that in most developed countries. The country that lowered its population growth would raise its standard of living 40 per cent above that of the other country in a single generation.

In terms of the gap between rich countries and poor, these studies show that it is the population explosion more than anything else which, by holding back the advancement of the poor, is blowing apart the rich and the poor and widening the already dangerous gap between them.

Furthermore, these recent economic studies show that this drag due to excessive population growth is quite independent of the density of population. This is something that needs emphasizing in view of the fact that many policy makers in the developing countries attach only minor importance to reducing population growth. It is a false claim that some countries need more population to fill their land or accelerate their economic growth. There are no vacant lands equipped with roads, schools, houses, and the tools of agricultural or industrial employment. Therefore, the people who are to fill those lands, before they can live at even the current low standard of living, must first eat up a portion of the present scarce supply of capital. It is this burden that defeats a nation's efforts to raise its standard of living by increasing its population.

No one can doubt then that very serious problems of population growth face most of the developing nations today. What are the chances of their being mastered by natural causes? The answer depends on our understanding the nature of the population explosion. It is caused not by an increase in the birth rate but by a dramatic drop in the death rate, due mainly to medical advances. It is this death control that has created the present emergency, and I do not believe that anyone would wish to reintroduce pestilence—or any other of the four horsemen of the apocalypse—as a "natural" solution to the population problem.

We are therefore faced with the question of what action we at the Bank, as a development agency, should take to lift this burden from the backs of many of our members. I propose the following three courses:

First: Let the developing nations know the extent to which rapid population growth slows down their potential development, and let them know that the optimum employment of the world's scarce development funds requires attention to this problem.

Second: Seek opportunities to finance facilities required by member countries to carry out family-planning programs.

Third: Join with others in programs of research to determine the most effective methods of family planning and of national administration of population control programs.

These three proposals for immediate action will, I hope, contribute to the success of the U.N. system, which is beginning to work in this field, and to the well-being of the developing nations.

Let me conclude by urging that, while we examine the innumerable and daunting problems that face all who exercise control over so much of the world's financial and economic power, none of us yield to despair as we see how much there is to do and how little time in which to do it.

There is no cause for despair. There is every reason for hope. In the past few generations the world has created a productive machine capable of abolishing poverty from the face of the earth. As we lift up our eyes from contemplating our troubles, who can fail to see the immense prospects that lie ahead for all mankind, if we have but the wit and the will to use our capacity fully?

I am not despondent about the difficulties that lie ahead, because I have faith in our ability to overcome them. That is why I have proposed a program of greatly increased activity by the World Bank, so that, by taking a lead in development assistance, we may encourage all who have begun to lose heart and slacken their pace—rich and poor alike.

If we in the Bank are able to double our efforts, this could be the signal for others to rally to the struggle, determined to use their overwhelming strength for the betterment of all mankind.

2

---◆---

The Population Issue:
Myths and Realities

My responsibilities as President of the World Bank compel me to be candid about the blunt facts affecting the prospects for global development. I have therefore chosen to speak publicly and often about the problem of excessive population growth. This problem is characterized by reticence and circumspection and yet is in desperate need of realism and candor. It is an issue so hypersensitive—and has given rise to such diverse opinions—that there is an understandable tendency simply to avoid argument, to turn one's attention to less complicated matters and hope that the problem will somehow disappear.

But the problem will not disappear.

What may disappear is the opportunity to find a solution

that is rational and humane. If we wait too long, that option will be overtaken by events. We cannot afford that. For if there is one thing certain about the population explosion, it is this: If it is not dealt with reasonably, it will in fact explode—explode in suffering and violence.

The most explosive fact of all is that the need for development is desperate. One-third of mankind today lives in an environment of relative abundance. But two-thirds of mankind—more than two billion individuals—remain entrapped in a cruel web of circumstances that severely limits their right to the necessities of life. They have not yet been able to achieve the transition to self-sustaining economic growth. They are caught in the grip of hunger and malnutrition, of high illiteracy and inadequate education, of shrinking opportunity and corrosive poverty.

The gap between the rich and poor nations is no longer merely a gap. It is a chasm. On one side are nations of the West that enjoy per capita incomes in the $3,000–$5,000 range. On the other are nations in Asia and Africa that struggle to survive on per capita incomes of less than $100.

What is important to understand is that this is not a static situation. The misery of the underdeveloped world is today a dynamic misery, continuously broadened and deepened by a population growth that is totally unprecedented in history. This is why the problem of population is an inseparable part of the larger, over-all problem of development.

There are some who speak as if simply having fewer people in the world is some sort of intrinsic value in and of itself. Clearly, it is not. But when human life is degraded by the plague of poverty, and that poverty is transmitted to future generations by too rapid a growth in population, then those with responsibilities in the field of development have no alternative but to deal with that issue.

To put it simply: The greatest single obstacle to the economic and social advancement of the majority of the peoples in the underdeveloped world is rampant population growth.

Having said that, let me make one point unmistakably clear: The solution of the population problem is in no way a substitute for the more traditional forms of developmental assistance, such as aid for the economic infrastructure, aid for agriculture, aid for industrialization, aid for education, and aid for technological advance. The underdeveloped world needs investment capital for a whole gamut of productive projects, but nothing would be more unwise than to allow these projects to fail because they are finally overwhelmed by a tidal wave of population.

Let us begin with the stark demographic dimensions. The dynamics are deceivingly simple. Population increase is merely the excess of births over deaths. For most of man's history, births and deaths have been in relative equilibrium. Only in the last century have they become seriously unbalanced.

Though the figures are well known, they are worth repeating, if for no other reason than to forestall the complacency that comes from too much familiarity with unpleasant facts. It required 1,600 years to double the world population of 250 million, as it stood in the first century A.D. Today, the more than 3 billion on earth will double in 35 years' time, and the world's population will then be increasing at the rate of an additional 1 billion every 8 years.

To project the totals beyond the year 2000 makes such a demand on the imagination as to render the statistics almost incomprehensible. A child born today, living on into his seventies, would know a world of 15 billion. His grandson would share the planet with 60 billion. In six and a half centuries—the same insignificant period of time separating us from the poet Dante—there would be one human being standing on every square meter of land on earth, a fantasy of horror that even the *Inferno* could not match.

Such projections are, of course, unreal. They will not come to pass because events will not permit them to come to pass. Of that we can be certain. What is not so certain is precisely what the nature of those events will be—mass starvation, political chaos, or reasonable population growth through population planning.

Regardless of what may happen after the year 2000, what is occurring right now is enough to jolt one into action. India, for example, is adding a million people a month to its population—and this in spite of the oldest family-planning program in Southeast Asia. The Philippines currently have a population of 41 million. In a brief 35 years at the present rate of growth, this limited island area will have to support over 100 million human beings. The average population growth of the world at large is 2 per cent. Many underdeveloped countries are burdened with a rate of 3.5 per cent or more. A population growing at 1 per cent doubles itself in 70 years; at 2 per cent it doubles in 35 years; at 3.5 per cent it doubles in only 20 years.

If we are to reject mass starvation and political chaos as solutions to this explosive situation, then there are clearly only three conceivable ways in which a nation can deliberately plan to diminish its rate of population growth: increase the death rate, step up the migration rate, or reduce the birth rate.

No one is in favor of the first choice. On the contrary, under the impact of public health programs, death rates are falling throughout the underdeveloped areas. Even simple medical improvements such as better sanitation, malaria suppression, and widespread vaccination bring on a rapid and welcome decline in mortality. The low-level death rates of

European nations, which it took a century and a half to achieve, are now being accomplished in the emerging areas in one-fifth of that time.

The second choice is wholly inadequate. Increased migration, on any scale significant enough to be decisive, is simply not practical. Countries concerned about their own future crowding are understandably disinclined to add to it by accepting more than a limited number of foreigners. But the more important point is that the continually expanding increment, on a global basis, is already so massive that migration as a solution to population pressure is manifestly unrealistic. We can put a man on the moon, but we cannot migrate, by the millions, off our own planet.

That leaves the third choice: a humane and rational reduction of the birth rate.

Is is feasible? It is. Is it simple? It is not. Is it necessary? Without question. It is necessary because the consequences of continuing the present population growth rates are unacceptable. Let us examine those consequences.

One cannot sense the inner significance of the cold, remote, impersonal demographic data by merely tracing a line upward on a graph or by scanning the printout from a computer. The consequences of rapid population growth—added to those of an already oppressive poverty—must be grasped in all their concrete, painful reality.

The first consequence can be seen in the gaunt faces of hungry men. One-half of humanity is hungering at this very moment. There is less food per person on the planet today than there was thirty years ago in the midst of a worldwide depression. Thousands of human beings will die today, as they die every day, of sheer hunger. Either they will starve to death or they will die because their diet is so inadequate that it cannot protect them from some easily preventable disease. Most of those thousands of individuals, whose intrinsic right to a decent life is as great as yours or mine, are children, not mere statistics. They are human beings. And they are dying. Now. They are not your children, or my children, but they are someone's children. And they are dying needlessly.

Yet the thousands who die are perhaps the more fortunate ones. For millions of other children, suffering the same malnutrition, do not die. They live languidly on, stunted in body and crippled in mind. The human brain reaches 90 per cent of its normal structural development in the first two years of life. We now know that during that critical period of growth, the brain is highly vulnerable to nutritional deficiencies. Such deficiencies can cause as much as 25 per cent impairment of normal mental ability. Even a deterioration of 10 per cent is sufficient to cause a serious handicap to productive life. This is irreversible brain damage.

What is particularly tragic in all of this is that when such mentally deprived children reach adulthood, they are likely to repeat the whole depressing sequence in their own families. They perpetuate mental deficiency, not through genetic inheritance but simply because, as parents, they are ill equipped to avoid the very nutritional deprivations in their own children that they themselves suffered.

Thus hunger and malnutrition forge a chain of conditions that causes human performance to spiral dismally downward. Alertness, vitality, energy, the ability to learn, the desire to succeed, the will to exert an effort—all these inestimable human qualities are drained away in the process. How many children today are caught up in this crisis? How many subsist at levels of hunger and malnutrition that practically guarantee that large numbers of them will be irreversibly mentally retarded for the rest of their lives? It is estimated that the total amounts to some 300 million.

But the population explosion's corrosive effects on the quality of life do not end with hunger. They range through the whole spectrum of human deprivation. With entire national populations already caught up in the dilemmas of development and doubling in some areas in as short a time as twenty years, there is a chronic insufficiency of virtually every necessity.

Current birth rates throughout the emerging world are seriously crippling developmental efforts. It is imperative to understand why. The irrefutable reason is that these governments must divert an inordinately high proportion of their limited national savings away from productive investment simply in order to maintain the current low level of existence for the expanding population.

Each additional child brought into the world must not only be fed but clothed, housed, medically cared for, and supported by at least minimal educational services. All of this requires new capital that cannot be invested in other desperately needed sectors of the economy. For approximately the first fifteen years of their lives, children cannot contribute economically to the nation, because they are consumers rather than producers.

If the number of children in the total population—as a result of high birth rates—is very large, a nation is under the compelling necessity to expend ever greater resources simply to keep its people from slipping beneath minimum subsistence levels. A treadmill economy tends to emerge, in which the total national effort will exhaust itself by running faster and faster merely to stand still. More and more classrooms must be built; more and more teachers must be provided; more and more vocational training facilities must be established. But despite all this effort, both the quantity and quality of education inevitably decline. It simply cannot keep pace with the mounting waves of children. Education, one of the prime movers of all human development, becomes the sacrificial victim.

As these ill-educated, perhaps wholly illiterate, children reach the age when they ought to become producers in the economy, they are engulfed by the hopelessness of under-employment. In many of the world's shantytowns 50 to 60 per cent of the adolescents are out of work. Not only are these youngsters not equipped for the jobs that might have been available, but the total number of meaningful jobs tends to decline in proportion to the population because the government has been unable to invest adequately in job-producing enterprises. Capital that ought to have been invested was not available. It had been dissipated by the ever rising tide of children.

This, then, is the cruel and self-perpetuating dilemma that governments face in developing countries that have been overburdened for long periods with high birth rates. Their plans for progress evaporate into massive efforts merely to maintain the status quo. What is true at the national level is repeated with even greater poignancy at the personal family level. Millions of families wish to avoid unwanted pregnancies, and when these families cannot find legal and compassionate assistance in this matter, they often turn to desperate and illegal measures.

Statistics suggest that abortion is one of the world's most commonly chosen methods to limit fertility, despite the fact that in many societies it is ethically offensive, illegal, expensive, and medically hazardous. In five countries of Western Europe, it is estimated that there are as many illegal abortions as live births. In India each month perhaps as many as a quarter of a million women undergo illegal abortion. In Latin America, illegal abortion rates are among the highest in the world. In one country, they are said to be three times the live birth rate; in another, to be the cause of two out of every five deaths of pregnant women. Further, there are indications that the illegal abortion rate in Latin America is increasing and that multiple illegal abortions are becoming common.

The tragic truth is that illegal abortion is endemic in many parts of the world. It is particularly prevalent in those areas where there is no adequate, organized family-planning assistance. The conclusion is clear: Where the public authorities will not assist parents to avoid unwanted births, the parents will often take matters into their own hands at whatever cost to conscience or health.

This entire question of population planning is incredibly complex. There are, of course, certain precise and painful moral dilemmas, but quite apart from these there is a vague and murky mythology that befogs the issue. Not only does this collection of myths obscure the essentials of the problem, but, worse still, it builds barriers to constructive action. I should like to turn now to that mythology, and examine some of its more irrational premises.

There is, to begin with, the generalized assumption that somehow "more people means more wealth." As with all fallacies, there is a deceptive substratum of plausibility to the thesis. With the rise of nationalism in the West—and the more recent emergence of newly independent countries in Asia and Africa—rapid population growth has often been regarded as a symbol of national vigor. It ensured (so it was believed) a more powerful military establishment, an economically advantageous internal market, a pool of cheap labor, and, in general, a prestigious political place in the sun.

In the underdeveloped world, nearly every one of these assumptions is false. Because rapid population growth tends seriously to retard growth in per capita income, the developing nation soon discovers that its economic vigor is diminished rather than enhanced by the phenomenon of high fertility. The hoped-for internal market becomes a mere mass of discontented indigents, without purchasing power but with all the frustrations of potential consumers whose expectations cannot be met.

"Cheap labor" in such countries turns out not to be cheap at all. Sound economic growth requires technological improvements, and these in turn demand higher levels of training than strained government resources can supply. Though individual workers may be paid lower salaries than their counterparts abroad, their efficiency and productiveness are so low that the nation's goods are often priced out of the competitive export market. The "cheap" labor turns out to be excessively expensive labor.

Even the argument of expanding the population in order to provide a powerful military force is suspect, not merely because the expansion of one nation's forces will, in time, lead to a reactive expansion of its neighbors' forces, but also because modern defense forces require an increasing ratio of educated recruits rather than masses of illiterate troops.

As for political prestige, nations caught in the catastrophe of an uncontrolled population growth do not enhance their position in the family of nations. On the contrary, they find it slipping away like their once optimistic plans for progress, to be replaced inevitably by the politics of confrontation and extremism.

Akin to the myth that "more people means more wealth" is the notion that countries with large tracts of uninhabited open land have no need to worry about birth rates, since there is ample room for expansion. The argument is as shallow as it is misleading. The patent fact is that mere open land does not, in and of itself, support a high rate of population growth. Such open land, if it is to become the home of large numbers of people, must be provided with a whole panoply of heavy government investments—investments in roads, in housing, in sanitation, and in agricultural and industrial development.

The sound economic argument is quite the other way round. What such raw space requires first is not surplus people but surplus funds for investment. And it is precisely surplus people in a developing economy that make the accumulation of surplus funds so incredibly difficult.

What is also overlooked is that a rational restraint on fertility rates in an emerging country never implies an absolute reduction of the total population. It merely presupposes a more reasonable balance between birth and death rates. And since death rates in the future are certain to drop with continued advances in medicine—and in highly underdeveloped countries the drop in the death rate is characteristically precipitous—there are no grounds whatever for fearing that a nation's population will dangerously ebb away under the influence of family planning. The danger is quite the opposite: that family planning will be inadequately utilized, and the population will proliferate to self-defeating levels.

A still more prevalent myth is the misapprehension that official programs of family planning in a developing country are wholly unnecessary since the very process of development itself automatically leads to lowered birth rates. The experience of Europe is cited as persuasive proof of this theory. But the proof is no proof at all, for the theory is hopelessly irrelevant to today's conditions in the underdeveloped world. There are no comparable circumstances between what happened in Europe's early period of modernization and what is happening in the emerging world today.

Aside from a lapse of logic, which fails to grasp that the current population growth in these areas inhibits the very economic development that is supposed to curb that growth, the historical fact is that conditions in Europe during its initial developmental period were far more favorable to lower rates of population growth. The birth rates were much lower than they are in the underdeveloped world today, the death rates had not yet drastically fallen, and by the time public health measures had accomplished that, the infrastructure of industrialization was already in place.

Further, in nineteenth-century Europe, marriages were entered into later than in the developing countries today, and the level of literacy, always an important factor in population growth, was considerably higher—in spite of which it required some seventy years for Europe to reduce its birth rates to present levels. Today the average birth rate for developing countries is 40 to 45 per 1,000 of population. To reduce this rate to the 17 to 20 per 1,000 that is common in contemporary Europe would require a reduction in the developing world of some 50 million births a year. To suppose that economic advancement by itself, without the assistance of well-organized family planning, could accomplish this in any feasible time frame of the future is wholly naïve.

Even with family planning, no such promising results are feasible in less than two or three decades. What is feasible—indeed, imperative—is the establishment of family planning on a scale that will stave off total economic and political disintegration in those countries where social progress is being seriously limited by the glut of unwanted births.

No government, of course, can succeed in convincing its own population to undertake family planning if parents themselves do not really want it, but the almost universal fact is that parents do want it. They often want it far more than their own political leaders comprehend. People—particularly poor, ill-educated people—may not understand the techniques of family planning. Most of them have only the most tenuous understanding of human biology. Often their limited comprehension is tragically confused by gross misinformation. But the notion that family-planning programs are sinister plots to coerce poor people into doing something they really do not want to do is absurd. The prevalence of voluntary illegal abortion should be enough to dispel that fiction. The poor do not always know how to limit their families in less drastic and dangerous ways, but there is overwhelming evidence that they would like to know how.

Another serious misunderstanding is the fear that family planning in the developing world would inevitably lead to a breakdown of familial moral fiber, and that it would encourage parents to limit the number of their children for essentially frivolous and selfish reasons, such as trading the responsibility of having a large number of children for the opportunity of acquiring the needless gadgetry of an advancing consumer economy.

A single stroll through the slums of any major city in the developing world is enough to dispel that concept. If anything is threatening the fiber of family life, it is the degrading conditions of subsistence survival that one finds in these sprawling camps of packing crates and scrap metal—children on the streets instead of in classrooms; broken men, their pride shattered, without work; despondent mothers, often unmarried, unable to cope with exhaustion because of annual pregnancies—all of this is a frustrating environment of misery and hunger and hopelesssness. These are not the conditions that promote an ethically strong family life. Family planning is not designed to destroy families, it is designed to save them.

All of us accept the principle that in a free society the parents themselves must determine the size of their own family. We would regard it as an intolerable invasion of the family's rights for the state to use coercive measures to implement population policy. We can preserve that right best by assisting families to understand how they can make that decision for themselves. Millions of children are born without their parents' desiring that it happen. Hence, a free, rational choice for an additional child is not made in these cases. If we are to keep the right of decision in the hands of the family, where it clearly belongs, we must give the family the knowledge and assistance required to exercise that right.

No one need be deterred from appropriate action by the pernicious, if pervasive, myth that the white Western world's assistance in family-planning efforts among the nonwhite nations of the developing areas is a surreptitious plot to keep the whites in racial ascendancy. The myth is absurd on purely demographic grounds, as well as on many others. Nonwhite peoples on the planet massively outnumber whites. They always have and always will. No conceivable degree of family planning could possibly alter that statistical truth.

If the white world actually did desire to plot against the nonwhite nations, one of the most effective ways to do so would be for the whites to deny these nations any assistance whatever in family planning. The progressive future of nations of the nonwhite world is directly related to their indigenous economic development, and that, in turn, as we have seen, is dependent upon their being able to reduce birth rates to a level that will allow a significant increase in per capita income.

One more myth obstructs the road to action. It is the belief that the time for decisive action is past, and that wholesale famine is inevitable. The distinguished British scientist and novelist C. P. Snow noted* that it is the view of men of sober judgment that "many millions of people in the poor countries are going to starve to death before our eyes. We shall see them doing so, on our television sets." He empha-

---

* In his "State of Siege" address to Westminster College, November 11 and 12, 1968, Fulton, Missouri; included in *The State of Siege* (New York: Scribner's, 1969).

sized that, when the collision between food and population takes place, "at best, this will mean local famines to begin with. At worst, the local famines will spread into a sea of hunger. The usual date predicted for the beginning of the local famines is 1975–80." In summing up, Snow predicted:

> The major catastrophe will happen before the end of the century. We shall, in the rich countries, be surrounded by a sea of famine, involving hundreds of millions of human beings.
>
> The increase of population all over the rich world may get a little less. In the poor world it won't, except in one or two pockets. Despite local successes, as in India, the food-population collision will duly occur. The attempts to prevent it, or meliorate it, will be too feeble. Famine will take charge in many countries. It may become, by the end of the period, endemic famine. There will be suffering and desperation on a scale as yet unknown.

Now, though Lord Snow is a brilliant and perceptive man of good will, I simply do not believe that one need feel quite so near despair, even in the face of a situation as ominous as this one. Wholesale famine is not inevitable. I am convinced that there is time to reverse the situation, if we will but use it. Only barely sufficient time, but time nevertheless. The time has been given us by those who have created the revolution in agricultural technology—a revolution based on new seeds, hybrid strains, fertilizers, and the intensified use of natural resources.

It is a revolution that already has increased the yields of food grains by more than 100 per cent in parts of Southeast Asia and that promises to boost yields by one-half ton per acre throughout Asia. It is a revolution which has expanded the number of acres sown with the new seeds from 200 in 1965 to 31 million in 1968—and an estimated 50.5 million in 1971—but which has yet to touch more than a small percentage of the rice- and wheat-producing acreage of the world.

If we will but speed the spread of this agricultural revolution by adequate and properly administered technical and financial assistance to the developing countries, we can expect that for the next two decades the world's food supply will grow at a faster rate than its population, and the predicted specter of famine can be averted. It will take immense energy and organizing skill and significant infusions of new capital investment, but such measures should make it possible to stave off disaster.

What is required to accomplish this is not so much a psychologically comforting optimism as an energetic, creative realism. I believe enough of that realism exists among men of good will—both in the developed and in the emerging world—to do the job. There is no point in being naïvely overoptimistic about an issue as full of peril as the population problem. But I am confident that application of the new technology will dramatically expand the rate of agricultural growth and will buy two decades of time—admittedly the barest minimum of time required to reduce the population explosion to manageable proportions.

How can this best be done?

To begin with, the developed nations must give every measure of support they possibly can to those countries that have already established family-planning programs. It is essential, of course, to recognize the right of a given country to handle its population problem in its own way, but handle the problem it must. The developed nations can point out the demographic facts. They can explain the economic realities and warn of the consequences of procrastination. They can, and should, inform. They should not, and cannot, pressure.

Technologically advanced countries can make one of their greatest contributions by initiating a new order of intensity in research into reproductive biology. Research facilities in this field have been starved for funds. The result is that we are still only on the threshold of understanding the complexities of conception and therefore only at the outer edge of the necessary knowledge to help make family planning in the developing countries beneficial on a meaningful scale. Research efforts should range far beyond biology. Demography, as a fully developed science, is still in its infancy. Probably fewer than half the world's births are even registered, and crude estimates of birth rates almost inevitably turn out to be too low, so it is essential that more precise data be developed in those areas where the population problem is the most acute.

Similarly, there is a pressing need for far more research in the socio-cultural aspects of family planning. There is manifestly a great deal more to population planning than birth control. Attitudes, motivation, and preferences differ from country to country, and this essential research can clearly best be conducted locally. The developed nations should be generous in their financial support for such studies and surveys.

Above all else, there is a need to develop a realistic sense of urgency in all countries over the population problem. Programs are beginning to show progress in limited areas, but no reduction in birth rates has yet been achieved anywhere in the underdeveloped areas that can significantly affect over-all world population totals. This means that family planning is going to have to be undertaken on a humane but massive scale. Other massive efforts in our century—in the field of public health, for example—have been mounted and have been successful. Granted all the difficulties, there is no reason whatever why this effort cannot also be successful.

The threat of unmanageable population pressures is very much like the threat of nuclear war. Both threats are undervalued. Both threats are misunderstood. Both threats can and will have catastrophic consequences unless they are dealt with rapidly and rationally. The threat of violence is intertwined with the threat of undue population growth. It is clear that population pressures in the underdeveloped societies can lead to economic tensions and political turbulence and cause stresses in the body politic that in the end can bring on conflicts among nations. This must not be allowed to happen. All of us share the responsibility of taking those actions necessary to ensure that it will not happen.

There need be no conflict with religious beliefs. The Roman Catholic Church, for example, is completely dedicated to the goal of development. One has only to read the Second Vatican Council's Pastoral Constitution on the Church in the Modern World, and Pope Paul's *Populorum Progressio*. Both these impressive documents call for a solution to the population problem as it relates to development. Such controversy as remains is about the means, not the end.

The end desired by the Church and by all men of good will is the enhancement of human dignity. That is what development is all about. Human dignity is threatened by the population explosion—more severely, more completely, more certainly threatened than it has been by any catastrophe the world has yet endured. There is time, just barely time, to escape that threat. We can and we must act.

What we must comprehend is this: The population problem will be solved one way or the other. Our only option is whether it is to be solved rationally and humanely—or irrationally and inhumanely. Is it to be solved by famine? By riot? By insurrection? By the violence that desperate, starving men are driven to? Are we to solve it by wars of expansion and aggression? Or are we to solve it rationally and humanely in accord with man's dignity?

There is so little time left to make the decision. To make no decision will be to make the worst decision of all. To ignore this problem is to make certain that nature will take catastrophic revenge on our indecisiveness. Providence has placed us at that point in history where a rational, responsible, moral solution to the population problem must be found. If we shirk that responsibility, we will have committed the ultimate crime, but it will be those who come after us who will pay the undeserved and unspeakable penalty.

3

---◆---

Major Development Problems: Malnutrition and Urban and Rural Unemployment

During my first year with the Bank, I visited Latin America, Asia, and Africa. I visited these areas in order to take a realistic look at their development problems at close range and to meet with the leaders who are grappling with the issues.

These trips and my regular subsequent visits strengthened my view that there are immense opportunities in the developing nations for high-priority, economically sound investment. At the same time, the complexities of development are so enormous that it would be naïve to suppose that more money alone can solve them. There is a desperate need for additional financial support, but there is at least as great a need for more effective use of the funds presently being provided. What we need and must fashion is a more effective over-all development strategy. That means investing our human and material resources in a carefully integrated manner that will contribute to the vitality, diversity, and basic institutional reform of developing societies. We cannot be satisfied with piecemeal solutions. We need a comprehensive strategy that will constitute an over-all plan into which particular policies and individual projects can be fitted as logical, integral parts. In brief, the situation as I see it is this:

• Economic development in the second half of this century is increasingly dominated by the consequences of rapid population growth. Mortality has fallen faster than fertility, and the effects of this disequilibrium require major changes in development policy if we are to achieve significant improvements in human welfare.

• In the long run, the most important issue is effective population planning. Its goal must be to stabilize the planet's population several decades earlier—and at a figure several billions lower—than it would otherwise be stabilized.*

---

* Recent demographic studies indicate that if a net reproduction rate of one (an average of two children per couple) is reached in the developing countries by the year 2040, a possible but by no means certain achievement, their present population of 2.6 billion will increase more than fivefold to nearly 14 billion before it levels off. If the net reproduction rate of one could be reached two decades sooner, the ultimate size of the population of the developing countries alone would be reduced by over 4 billion, a figure substantially in excess of the planet's total population today.

	Developed Countries	Developing Countries	Total World
Present Population (in billions)	1.1	2.6	3.7
Ultimate Population (in billions)			
If replacement rate is reached by developing countries in 2040 and developed countries in 2020	1.8	13.9	15.7
If replacement rate is reached two decades earlier	1.6	9.6	11.2

(Footnote continued on page 50)

• Since reducing birth rates to replacement levels will necessarily require decades, we must reshape development programs now, in order to take account of what is certain to be a continuing, rapid growth of population to levels heretofore considered unlikely. Two of the consequences of such growth—widespread malnutrition and chronic and growing unemployment—require particular attention.

• It is clear that malnutrition prevents realization of the full genetic potential of hundreds of millions of persons in the developing world and retards both economic and social development. But research has pointed out feasible means to make immediate progress on this neglected problem.

• The problems of unemployment and underemployment are already severe and will become worse as the rate of growth of the labor force accelerates in the two or three decades ahead.

• Poverty, inequality, and unemployment cannot be effectively dealt with by expanding the urban sector alone but must be attacked directly in the rural areas through measures which will raise the incomes of the poorer farmers and the landless.

The truth is that development programs have not as yet faced up to the adjustments that the consequences of continuing population growth require. The profound concern we must feel for the rapid growth of population stems precisely from the menace it brings to any morally acceptable standard of existence. To quote the more extreme critics of population policy, we do not want fewer children born into the world because we do not like their color or fear their future enmity or suspect that they will in some unspecified way encroach upon the high consumption standards of

---

Two important conclusions can be drawn from the above projections: Each decade of delay in addressing the population problem in developing countries will lead to an ultimate population in those nations approximately 20 per cent larger than would otherwise be the case; even on very favorable assumptions, the populations of the developing countries will continue to grow rapidly for several decades, expanding perhaps fourfold from present levels and reaching a total of nearly 10 billion.

already industrialized lands. Population control is not, as is sometimes claimed, an exercise in concealed genocide, perpetrated by the already rich on the aspiring poor. It has one source and one only—the belief that without a slowing down and control of the population explosion, the life awaiting millions upon millions of this planet's future inhabitants will be stunted, miserable, and tragic—or, if you prefer the hackneyed but apt adjectives used by the philosopher Hobbes, "nasty, brutish, and short."

This undeniable fact takes us far beyond the population explosion. We have to see the population problem as part— a vital, critical part but still only a part—of a much wider social and political crisis that grows deeper with each decade and threatens to round off this century with years of unrest and turbulence, a "time of troubles" during which the forces of historical change threaten our frail twentieth-century society with disintegration.

We cannot divert these forces. They are an essential part of the process by which mankind is adapting the whole of its life to the advances in science and technology. About one-third of humanity has moved far in the transfer toward modernization and relative affluence. The rest of the human species jostle behind. They certainly have no intention of renouncing the wealth, prosperity, and, above all, the power locked up in modern technology.

"Modernization" is a primary objective of still developing nations, but they are seeking to modernize under quite unprecedented conditions. Technological and scientific modernization is now more complicated and more hazardous than it was for the industrial nations a century ago. This is the real root of the crisis.

Mr. Lester Pearson in a speech at the Columbia University Conference on International Economic Development in February, 1970, gave a cogent and relevant resume of the historical differences between nineteenth- and twentieth-century development. He emphasized the contrast between the balanced and fundamentally progressive character of economic, social, and technological change in the nineteenth century and the growing evidence of fundamental imbalance and, hence, regressive forces at work in the unfolding of the same processes of modernization today.

In the nineteenth century, population—held down by epidemics and poor public health—caused the work force to grow by less than 1 per cent per year. This was just about the amount that the technology of the times could usefully absorb and employ. Agricultural productivity rose, and land was opened up for European use all around the globe. The cities grew as centers of manufacturing. By the time technology demanded fewer but more sophisticated workers, and public health had lowered the death rate, education and city living had produced a more stable population. The vast migration of Europeans to new lands was an additional safety valve.

Today, every one of the nineteenth-century conditions is reversed. Advances in public health have resulted in a growth of population which increases the work force by at least 2 per cent per year. At the same time, technology becomes steadily more capital-intensive and absorbs steadily fewer men. Although agricultural productivity is now on the rise, the new techniques are destabilizing in the sense that they widen income inequities and release still more workers from the overcrowded land.

So the cities fill up and urban unemployment steadily grows. Very probably there is an equal measure of worklessness in the countryside. The poorest quarter of the population in developing lands is left almost entirely behind in the vast transformation toward the modern technological society.

The "marginal" men, the wretched strugglers for survival on the fringes of farm and city, may already number more than half a billion. By 1980 their number may surpass one billion; by 1990, two billion. Can we imagine any human order surviving with so gross a mass of misery piling up at its base?

At least a quarter of the human race faces the prospect of entering the twenty-first century in poverty more unacceptable than that of any previous epoch. Frankly I do not see this as a situation in which any of our shared hopes for a long peace and steady material progress are likely to be achieved. On the contrary, I agree with Lester Pearson's contention that "a planet cannot, any more than a country, survive, half-slave, half-free, half-engulfed in misery, half-careening along towards the supposed joys of almost unlimited consumption." In that direction lies disaster, yet that is our direction today unless we are prepared to change course—and to do so in time.

How then should we react to this threat of impending catastrophe? I must assume that we will react, for to carry on any of our activities as political leaders, government officials, business or labor leaders, or responsible citizens, we must take for granted the existence of a certain minimum rationality in human affairs. It is not rational to confront pressures far greater than those of the revolutionary periods of the eighteenth and nineteenth centuries without accepting the consequences.

Today, in the developing world:

Malnutrition is common.
The Food and Agriculture Organization estimates that at least a third to a half of the world's people suffer from hunger or nutritional deprivation. The average person in a high-standard area consumes four pounds of food a day as compared with an average pound and a quarter in a low-standard area.

Infant mortality is high.

Infant deaths per 1,000 live births are four times as high in the developing countries as in the developed countries (110 compared with 27).

Life expectancy is low.

A man in the West can expect to live 30 per cent longer than the average man in the developing countries and twice as long as the average man in some African countries.

Illiteracy is widespread.

There are 100 million more illiterates today than there were twenty years ago, bringing the total to some 800 million.

Unemployment is endemic and growing.

The equivalent of approximately 20 per cent of the entire male labor force is underemployed or unemployed, and in many areas the urban population is growing twice as fast as the number of urban jobs.

The distribution of income and wealth is severely skewed.

In India, 12 per cent of the rural families control more than half of the cultivated land. In Brazil, less than 10 per cent of the families control 75 per cent of the land. The gap between the per capita incomes of the rich nations and the poor nations is widening rather than narrowing, both relatively and absolutely. At the extremes that gap is already more than $4,000. Present projections indicate it may well widen to $9,000 by the end of the century. In the year 2000, per capita income in the United States is expected to be approximately $10,000; in Brazil, $500; and in India, $200.

Just how much worse these conditions were at the end of the 1960's than at the beginning is difficult to determine. For most of them, even today, we lack satisfactory indicators and data. The result is that trying to plan to improve these conditions is like trying to plan price stabilization without price indices. It is a nearly impossible task.

The lesson to be learned is that in setting the objectives, planning the programs, and measuring the progress of development in the 1970's we must look to more than gross measures of economic growth. What we require are relevant "development indicators" that go beyond the measure of growth in total output and provide practical yardsticks of change in the other economic, social, and moral dimensions of the modernizing process. To limit our attention to expanding GNP, even though it be from 5 per cent per year to 6 or 7 per cent, can only lead to greater political, social, and economic disequilibrium. However important an increase in GNP may be as a necessary condition of development, it is not a sufficient condition.

This is not to say that the target of the Second Development Decade—reaching a 6 per cent annual growth rate of GNP for the developing world in the 1970's—is not both feasible and necessary. But if we achieve the "quantity" goals, and neglect the "quality" goals of development, we will have failed. It is as simple as that.

The Second Development Decade gives us the opportunity to establish and pursue quality goals of development with new insights, new strategies, and new emphases. But—and I repeat the point—we cannot content ourselves with the mere quantity of our operations if they are not adding to the genuine quality of man's life on the planet. And if our investments are to meet this wider goal, I frankly admit that we and other investors need to add to the patterns of analysis a new dimension of social concern.

Consider, for example, the problem of malnutrition. Much of the most significant knowledge dealing with nutritional deficiencies—and most particularly their implications for development—has been discovered only recently. Even now the full extent of these deficiencies in the developing countries and the degree to which they seriously limit economic and social progress are only beginning to become apparent. We have hardly even begun to develop plans to deal with the problem.

Malnutrition is in fact widespread. It is a major cause of high mortality among young children. It limits the physical, often the mental, growth of hundreds of millions of those who survive and reduces their productivity as adults. Malnutrition is therefore a major barrier to human development. Yet, despite the evidence that with a relatively small per capita expenditure of resources major gains can be achieved, there is scarcely a country in the developing world where a concerted attack on the problem is under way.

The number of childhood deaths is enormous in the poorer countries. Malnourishment severely lowers immunity to infection, and tens of millions of children succumb each year to preventable fatalities simply because they have no reserves of resistance. The Food and Agriculture Organization states that "malnutrition is the biggest single contributor to child mortality in the developing countries." That contention is borne out by the Pan American Health Organization's reports of studies in Latin America that show malnutrition to be either the primary cause of—or a major contributing factor in—50 to 75 per cent of the deaths of one- to four-year-olds.

How great is child mortality in typical countries in the developing world?

- In India, there are large areas where deaths in the first year of life number as many as 150 to 200 per 1,000 live births.

- In Egypt, the proportion of children between the ages of one and two who die is more than 100 times higher than in Sweden.

- In Cameroon, children under five, although only one-sixth of the population, account for one-half of the deaths.

- In Pakistan and Bangladesh, the percentage of children between the ages of one and four who die is forty times higher than in Japan.

Clearly, the principal result of widespread malnutrition is

high child mortality.* But not all malnourished children die. Hundreds of millions of those who live (and the Food and Agriculture Organization and the World Health Organization estimate that as many as two-thirds of all surviving children in the developing countries have been malnourished) suffer serious deprivation of the opportunity to realize their full human potential.

The deprivation often begins before the child is born. While it is difficult to distinguish the effects of protein deficiency on child development from other aspects of poverty in the child's environment, there can be no serious doubt that there is a relationship between severe malnutriton in infancy and mental retardation (which more and more scientists are concluding is irreversible). Autopsies have revealed that young children who die of protein-calorie malnutrition may have less than half the number of brain cells of adequately nourished children in the same age group. Protein deficiency also limits physical growth to a serious extent. The director of the National Institute of Nutrition in India reports that 80 per cent of the nation's children suffer from "malnutrition dwarfism." Low-income populations almost universally have a smaller body size. The Food and Agriculture Organization estimates that more than 300 million children from these groups suffer grossly retarded physical growth.

Prolonged into adulthood, the poor mental and physical growth characteristics of the early years can greatly impair the range of human capacities. Add to that the current low standards of nutrition for grown adults in much of the developing world, and it is clear why there are adverse effects

* It is becoming clear that the population problem and the nutrition problem are closely intertwined. In the end, better nutrition will have a beneficial effect on reducing fertility, despite the short-run reduction in infant mortality. Indeed, many authorities believe that reduced infant and child mortality are preconditions for successful population control.

on the ability to work. Workers who are easily fatigued and have low resistance to chronic illness not only are inefficient, but help substantially to increase the accident rate, the incidence of absenteeism, and unnecessary medical expenditures. More serious still, to the extent that their mental capacity has been impaired by malnutrition in childhood, their ability to perform technical tasks is reduced. Dexterity, alertness, initiative—these are the qualities that malnutrition attacks and diminishes.

We are not speaking here of dietetic nuances or the fancies of food faddists. We are speaking of basic nutritional deficiencies that affect the minds and bodies of human beings. The problem is so dimly perceived and so readily dismissed under the pressure of other priorities that we have neither applied the knowledge now at hand nor mobilized the resources required to broaden that knowledge.

In one sense, of course, the basic cause of malnutrition is poverty, but this does not mean that we must, or can even afford to, wait for full economic development to take place before we begin to attack the problem. On the contrary, reducing the ravages of serious malnutrition will itself accelerate economic development and thus contribute to the amelioration of poverty. There are a number of practical steps that can be taken even within the limitations of our current knowledge and economic priorities.

As in the case of the population problem, the nutrition problem represents less a need for new and immense amounts of development capital than a need for realistic understanding of the situation. What we already know suggests that to meet basic nutritional deficiencies of hundreds of millions of the peoples of the developing countries will not entail unacceptable costs. It has been estimated, for example, that for $8 per child per year, we could make up the deficiencies of a diet that now deprives him of one-fourth of his protein need and one-third of his caloric need.

There are many promising low-cost agricultural and industrial solutions to the problem of increasing the nutritional value of food:

● Crop shifts—through appropriate pricing policies—from low-protein cereals to high-protein pulses.

● The introduction of higher nutritive strains of conventional cereals, such as the new high-lysine corn which doubles protein value.

● The fortification of existing basic foods to improve their nutritional value, such as the protein fortification of cereals and the vitamin and iron fortification of wheat flour.

● The development and distribution of wholly new low-cost processed foods, particularly for the feeding of young children, using available oilseed protein.

There are, of course, many other solutions deserving of support. Some are already available, some near at hand on the research horizon, but none of them is going to work if the international development community and the governments of the countries concerned fail to face up to the importance and implications of the nutrition problem.

Another serious consequence of the population explosion is unemployment. The fall in the death rates, which caused the population explosion in developing countries, disproportionately affected the youngest age groups, with the result that the major increase in population occurred initially among children under the age of fifteen. The growth in the labor force (age fifteen and over) has been slower but is now accelerating. Between 1950 and 1960, it rose 1.6 per cent compared with a population growth rate of 2.3 per cent. In the period 1960–70, the figure was roughly 1.9 per cent compared with 2.6 per cent.

Throughout the developing world the labor force will grow at an even faster rate in the 1970's than it did in the 1960's. On average, it will rise 2.3 per cent per year. And when one reflects on the expected 2.8 per cent growth in population for the next decade, it is clear that labor-force growth rates for the developing world as a whole will inevitably accelerate in the two or three decades immediately ahead. In Latin America these rates are already over 3 per cent.

What these figures mean for some of the principal countries is staggering. It is estimated, for example, that the Indian labor force will grow by over 50 million in the next ten years. This is equivalent to the combined labor force of Great Britain and the Federal Republic of Germany.

These rates of growth are far higher than the 1–1.5 per cent per year faced by the developing countries of Western Europe a century ago. Those growth rates could readily be relieved by massive emigration to the then underpopulated New World with its abundant natural resources. No such large-scale relief is available for today's developing countries.

Available statistics and concepts of employment and unemployment are both inadequate and ambiguous in developing countries. However, there is ample evidence that, although growth rates of national product have increased substantially over the past decade, very few developing economies have expanded fast enough to absorb the growth in their labor force. Today I believe most economists would agree that (1) unemployment and underemployment are extremely serious in the developing countries, much more so than in the developed countries; (2) by any reasonable definition—and making allowances for underemployment—unemployment approximates 20–25 per cent in most developing countries; and

(3) if past patterns continue, unemployment is bound to become worse.*

It can be misleading to speak of the employment problem. There are in fact two distinct employment problems: one urban and one rural. Of the two, the urban problem is usually the more dramatic. Estimates of total open unemployment in most developing countries are in the range of 5 to 10 per cent of the total labor force, but, as this unemployment is very heavily concentrated in cities, the proportion of the urban labor force that is unemployed is much greater.

Urban surveys in the 1960's showed unemployment to be widespread in many developing countries. In the urban areas of Algeria it was 27 per cent and in the Philippines 13 per cent; and in Bogotá, Colombia, 16 per cent. The age group the Ivory Coast 20 per cent; in Kingston, Jamaica, 19 per cent; and in Bogotá, Colombia, 16 per cent. The age group most adversely affected was the 15- to 24-year-olds. Nearly 40 per cent of this age group in Ceylon's urban labor force was unemployed in 1968. Such massive unemployment among youth carries with it a very heavy social cost. The opportunity to acquire productive skills and steady work habits at the

* The following table prepared by the International Labor Organization, while suffering from the weaknesses affecting all such estimates, illustrates the magnitude of the problem. It projects an increase of 170 million in the labor force during the decade 1970–80, with only half as great an increase in the number of full-time jobs.

Levels of Unemployment and Underemployment in Developing Countries, Excluding Mainland China

	1970	1980	1970		1980	
	Millions		Per cent		Per cent	
Fully employed	504	592	75.3		70.5	
Underemployed	130	200	19.4		23.8	
Employed	634	792	94.7	24.7	94.3	29.5
Unemployed	36	48	5.3		5.7	
Total Labor Force	670	840	100.0		100.0	

most receptive age is lost, and a corrosive social frustration is created that can ultimately erupt into open and irrational violence.

Underemployment is also common in urban areas. Far more people eke out a meager living in unproductive and excessively duplicated service activities than are actually required by the volume of work performed. While it is impossible to measure precisely the extent of this phenomenon, the proportion of the nonagricultural labor force engaged in services in most Latin American countries, for example, is between 60 and 70 per cent and tending to rise, whereas in the developed countries of Europe it has been generally constant for several decades at between 40 and 50 per cent.

As bad as the urban situation is, almost everywhere the rural underemployment problem is numerically worse. Since it involves the poorest people of a developing society, it is even more tragic. Typically it results from large families sharing the little work provided by tiny farms or from landless laborers able to find jobs only at peak seasons of the year. The result is an immense waste of potentially productive resources. It has been estimated that in Latin America in 1960 rural underemployment amounted to the equivalent of one-third of the agricultural labor force. This is likely to have risen since then.

Even more important than this waste of resources is the cost of underemployment in terms of human misery. The problem is not only that people are unoccupied for so much of the year but that the employment they can find yields them so little income. In Brazil the poorest 20 per cent, who are predominantly rural, had in 1960 an average income only one-sixth of the national average. Recent studies indicate that between 40 and 50 per cent of the population of India currently have incomes below a poverty line nationally established in terms of basic nutritional needs. These studies suggest that the situation has worsened rather than improved in recent years.

Rural underemployment is a major cause of the large and often widening gap between urban and rural incomes. In most developing countries, average incomes in the urban areas are far higher than in the rural areas. In metropolitan Manila, for example, the average income is almost four times that of rural areas in the Philippines.

Rural and urban unemployment are clearly related. To many in the countryside it appears more attractive to migrate to the cities, even without work, in the hope of finding eventual employment, than it is to endure the poverty of underemployment in agriculture. Although there is a good deal that can and must be done to increase the rate of growth in productive jobs in the urban areas—as I will discuss later—so long as rural underemployment exists, the income gap will exist, and the number of rural poor migrating to cities will tend to exceed the number of new jobs there. Solving the urban problem therefore depends on solving the rural problem. And the solution to the rural problem must be found mainly in the rural areas. There is no hope, in most countries, that urban job creation will be fast enough to absorb all the underemployed from the countryside.

For employment to grow at a rate of 4.5 per cent per year in the urban areas of the developing world would be a tremendous achievement, beyond anything that has been achieved in the past. Growth of manufacturing employment in developing countries between 1955 and 1965 approximated 4 per cent, with growth of manufacturing output of over 7 per cent; and in all regions of the world the gap between these rates was tending to widen. The bulk of the population of the developing world is in countries with at least 70 per cent of the people now living in rural areas. In such countries, a 4.5 per cent growth in urban jobs would provide work for an increase to the total rural and urban labor force of 1.3 per cent, or approximately one-half of the increase anticipated. The remainder must be accommodated in the rural sector, already characterized by heavy underemployment.

Development programs that place the relief of poverty, the elimination of malnutrition, and jobs for the unemployed high among their goals must therefore give prime attention to agriculture. It is in the nature of the growth process, however, that the relative importance of agriculture in every economy declines as economic development proceeds. As people grow richer, they spend a smaller proportion of their income on food and more on manufactured goods and services. As technology advances, proportionately fewer resources go into producing raw materials and proportionately more into processing these materials into increasingly sophisticated manufactured goods.

The realization that at a later stage in a given society agriculture will gradually lose its primacy to other sectors does not justify neglecting it at an earlier stage. But this is just what is happening in many cases today. Public investment often favors urban areas; trade policies, exchange-rate policies, and price policies often discriminate against agriculture. Excessive export taxes and rigid price controls restrict farm earnings, and squeeze the farmer who has to buy manufactured inputs and consumer goods from protected high-cost domestic industries.

Eight years ago drought on the Indian subcontinent awakened the world to the precariousness of its food supply. Asian prospects appeared particularly grim. Though drought is, and will remain in rain-fed areas, a serious threat, progress in Asian cereal production has been dramatic enough to justify the term "revolution." This so-called Green Revolution, however, has been primarily a revolution in the production of wheat, rice, and maize, and it has been largely confined to irrigated agriculture. So far, its impact has been massively felt in only a few countries, principally India, Pakistan, and the Philippines.

The Green Revolution has not solved the long-term world food problems, but it has given us confidence that they can be solved. It has reminded us that, once man is persuaded of the urgency of the task, his ability to solve technological problems is immense. In the same spirit, we have to see the social and economic problems of development—where mankind's record so far has been less impressive—as challenges rather than as causes for discouragement.

The need to sustain the momentum of the Green Revolution and to meet the rural employment and income problems continues to provide such challenges, both technological and socio-economic. At present, the new technology requires irrigation, but over 75 per cent of India's arable land and about 60 per cent of Pakistan's are without irrigation. To benefit the majority of farmers, technological research on new varieties suitable for nonirrigated agriculture is essential.

Further agricultural research is needed in all parts of the developing world. Little research is going on for certain important crops—tubers, for example, and high-yielding pulses —and little research is going on in certain important regions— the deep-water rice areas, for example, of the Ganges River and Mekong Delta. Developed countries normally spend very much more on agricultural research in relation to the size of the sector than do the developing countries. The United States, Israel, and Australia spend on agricultural research the equivalent of between 2 and 3 per cent of the agricultural commodity value; Japan and northern Europe spend about 1 per cent. But the developing countries of Asia and Latin America spend only about one-tenth to four-fifths of 1 per cent of agriculture's commodity value.

Because of the immense importance of this type of research,

the Bank has taken a new step, and has joined with the Food and Agriculture Organization and the United Nations Development Program to sponsor an international consultative group to mobilize finance in order to continue and expand the work of existing international research centers and to establish new ones.*

If we are to meet the social and economic challenge implicit in the Green Revolution, we must find ways to prevent its benefits from being monopolized by wealthier farmers. So far, the more advantaged farmers have obtained disproportionate shares of irrigation water, fertilizers, seeds, and credit. Unwise financial policies have sometimes encouraged these farmers to carry out excessive mechanization. Farm machinery has been made available at too cheap a price by allowing equipment to be imported at overvalued exchange rates and purchased with loans bearing unrealistically low interest rates.

This is not to argue that farm mechanization in countries with rural employment problems is always unwise. Sometimes it may increase employment by multiplying the crop cycles during the year. In itself the Green Revolution should lead to an increase in employment per acre through increasing output by encouraging double-cropping and through stimulating the development of ancillary agricultural activities, but this benefit can be offset by excessive mechanization.

The benefits of agricultural progress may also be limited if its effect is that the already more advantaged large farmers expand at the expense of sharecroppers and small farmers. In India and Pakistan, agricultural incomes are largely

* The Consultative Group on International Agricultural Research held its first meeting in May, 1971. There were five research centers at that time. Since then, the International Crops Research Institute for the Semi-Arid Tropics (ICRISAT) has been established in India, and the International Laboratory for Research on Animal Diseases (ILRAD) is being established in Kenya.

exempt from direct taxation, and large farmers have used their windfall profits to enlarge their farms even further. In contrast, the Republic of China imposes a 7-acre limit on farm size in Taiwan, and agricultural development has in consequence been relatively labor-intensive.

What is frequently forgotten is that small farmers often work their holdings more intensively than large farmers and often achieve a higher output per acre. Research in Colombia has shown that if land, labor, and capital are given prices appropriate to their relative scarcities, farms smaller than 25 acres can be economically more efficient than substantially larger farms. Studies in India and Brazil have produced similar findings.

All this suggests that there are many communities in which the reasonable redistribution of land, currently held in excessively large blocks, to the landless or to small farmers would be desirable not only on grounds of equity, but on grounds of efficiency as well. Land redistribution by itself, however, is not likely to lead to more output unless those who receive it are also given the necessary assistance to finance and improve farming techniques. This will require a change in the structure of credit institutions and extension services, which typically serve large farmers.

If the poorer farmers do not benefit from the Green Revolution's increase in output, they cannot increase their own food consumption, and the whole drive toward greater productivity will be diminished by a sluggish market. Conversely, an increased availability of food and income to large segments of the rural population could well be self-reinforcing and boost labor productivity. It would also provide an opportunity for countries to utilize their unemployed through rural investment in transport, schools, clinics, and irrigation —and without the costs of food imports or inflation. Experience with such programs on the Asian subcontinent and in

Tunisia during the 1960's was encouraging, and India has recently begun to blueprint a new program of rural works.

The measures I have outlined here suggest that there need be no necessary economic conflict between the goal of helping the mass of the rural population and other goals of economic development. Land reform and practical assistance for the small farmer will benefit those who can get the highest output from the scarcest factor—land. Realistic prices for productive factors, and for output, will not only help to maximize total output, but will tend to increase employment as well. Rural works will serve to build up rural infrastructure and to raise incomes.

Recent projects financed by the Bank have been directed expressly to an integrated approach to rural development that will benefit small farmers. But we have to admit that in this whole area we are still feeling our way. None of us in the Bank or in the development community at large can yet presume that we are experts at designing the most effective institutions for helping small farmers, or that we know enough about the use of labor-intensive methods of construction, or how best to launch large-scale rural works programs. All these matters manifestly need further study and experimentation.

These issues are fully as urgent as the proper exchange rates or optimal mixes of the factors of production. The only trouble is that we do not know enough about them. I would go further and say that, up to a point, we do not even know how to think about them. Just as the censuses of the 1950's helped to alert us to the scale of the population explosion, the urban and employment crises of the 1960's are alerting us to the scale of social displacement and general uprootedness of populations that are exploding not only in numbers but in movement as well. But we are still only picking up the distress signals. We still do not know how to act.

We should be frank about this. In field after field, we have more questions than answers. Our urgent need is for new instruments of research and analysis that will dispel our ignorance of the social dimensions of economic change and help us formulate a more comprehensive strategy for the decade ahead.

We in the World Bank cannot, of course, alone and from our own resources, provide all the new information and expertise required, but we can stimulate and be part of a wider research and education effort, and we can help draw together new resources for the formulation of wise development policies. We propose to seek the cooperation of universities, foundations, research units, and other international institutions and their experienced administrators for that purpose.

Further, to provide a solid foundation for consultation and action by both developed and developing nations in the whole field of development strategy and administration of aid, we have planned and are now putting into effect a new and expanded program of Country Economic Missions. These will be regularly scheduled, thoroughly staffed, comprehensive missions whose mandate will be to assist the member government to draw up an over-all development strategy that will include every major sector of the economy. The missions will be looking into not only the traditional problems of economic growth but the other facets of development as well: questions related to such issues as population increase, urbanization, land reform, income distribution, public health, and environmental preservation. Once the mission is completed, we will promptly produce for use by all of the parties concerned a thorough Economic Report which will serve as a profile of the country's progress and of its over-all development plan. The essential point is that it will be comprehensive in scope and regular in schedule and will form the basis for strategic rather than merely tactical development financing.

Perhaps one of the most wasteful mistakes that both developing countries and aid agencies can make is to proceed on a random project-by-project basis, without first establishing an over-all development strategy and then selecting projects that mutually support and interlock with one another within that over-all plan. Our new program for Country Economic Reports is designed to provide a foundation for such a strategy.

All of us within the worldwide community have a mandate in common. Our ultimate goals are to help build the planet into a more habitable home for mankind and to help create a political, social, and economic environment in which men and women can more freely develop their own highest potential.

The funds we require to accomplish this are infinitesimal compared with the funds the wealthy nations are already devoting to prodigiously disproportionate objectives. The talents and managerial skills we require are at hand. We need only to organize them.

Finally, the most important ingredient of all—the dedication, the drive, the determination to see the task through—is, I believe, within reach. If development becomes a social as well as an economic objective, if it aims squarely at an end to grinding poverty and gross injustice, I believe it has a constituency waiting for it among the emerging generation of young adults. These young men and women are looking for goals beyond personal affluence. Development is surely a challenge that can command their dedication, provided it is concerned not simply with goods and gadgets but with the self-respect and dignity of man.

Those, I believe, are the true dimensions of the task that lies before all of us in the Second Decade of Development.

4

---◆---

Financing Development: The Relationship of Aid, Trade, and Industrial Expansion

I have stressed the importance of agricultural and rural development because it is in the countryside and on the land that the great mass of the people live in the developing world. But even under the best of circumstances agricultural employment will not be able to grow fast enough to absorb the growing rural labor force, which is an inevitable result of the population explosion.

The drift to the cities of the landless and the jobless is bound to increase. Today the major cities are doubling in size roughly every decade. By the year 2000 their total population will be some 500 per cent higher than today. More than a billion people will be seeking to make a living in these sprawling centers of urban decay.

Only a vast expansion of industry can begin to provide jobs for a proportion of these people. Furthermore, only industry can provide that rapid economic growth which is essential if the standard of living of the growing population is to be maintained, let alone improved.

Finally, industrial growth is essential if the developing countries are to obtain a larger share of world trade with their exports and thus earn the foreign exchange they so desperately need to buy the tools of development from the already industrialized world. Their need for foreign exchange and the extent to which aid and trade may supply it is the subject of this chapter.

The target for the Second Development Decade, adopted by the United Nations General Assembly in 1970, calls for an average GNP growth rate of 6 per cent during the 1970's. This acceleration of economic growth over the 5 per cent rate achieved in the 1960's will require that imports grow more rapidly than national income. This explains why the U.N. General Assembly calls for an annual increase of approximately 7 per cent in the imports of the developing countries during the 1970's.

Foreign exchange requirements will grow faster than this. Developing countries have had to borrow an increasing proportion of such requirements. The result has been a rapid rise in obligations for the servicing of this debt in the form of amortization and interest. The Bank's projections indicate that these borrowings will lead to an increase in debt service substantially exceeding the rate of increase of national income. In other words, in order to attain a rate of import growth close to 7 per cent and meet their debt obligations, de-

veloping countries will require foreign exchange resources to
grow by over 7 per cent a year.

The foreign exchange shortage of the developing countries
is made more desperate by the shortfall in Official Development Assistance (ODA), which is aid on concessionary, very
low interest terms. The developed countries, in adopting the
strategy for the Second Development Decade and in support
of the growth target, stated that the level of external aid to
be provided in the form of Official Development Assistance
should reach .7 per cent of their GNP's by 1975.

Where do we stand today in that effort?

A number of the developed countries have made significant
progress toward this objective as the table below indicates:

PROJECTED FLOW OF OFFICIAL DEVELOPMENT ASSISTANCE *
MEASURED AS A PER CENT OF GROSS NATIONAL PRODUCT

	1970	1971	1972	1973	1974	1975
Australia	.59	.52	.59	.59	.59	.60
Austria	.13	.06	.17	.19	.22	.25
Belgium	.48	.49	.54	.58	.62	.66
Canada	.42	.37	.42	.44	.45	.47
Denmark	.38	.43	.48	.53	.58	.64
France	.68	.68	.65	.65	.65	.65
Germany	.32	.34	.33	.36	.36	.38
Italy	.16	.17	.16	.16	.16	.16
Japan	.23	.23	.28	.32	.36	.40
Netherlands	.63	.60	.70	.74	.76	.78
Norway	.32	.33	.47	.56	.67	.75
Portugal	.61	.75	.45	.45	.45	.45
Sweden	.36	.45	.50	.56	.65	.71
Switzerland	.15	.12	.22	.26	.30	.32
United Kingdom	.37	.41	.41	.41	.45	.46
United States	.31	.32	.30	.28	.26	.24
Average	.34	.35	.36	.36	.36	.37

* Countries included are members of the Development Assistance Com-
mittee of the Organization for Economic Cooperation and Development,
accounting for more than 95 per cent of total Official Development Assistance. Figures for 1970 and 1971 are actual data. The projections for
later years are based on World Bank estimates of growth of GNP, on
information on budget appropriations for aid, and on aid policy state-

However, on the basis of present indications, only three countries (the Netherlands, Norway, and Sweden) will reach or exceed the target. Four more countries (Australia, Belgium, Denmark, and France) will come close. Four others will substantially increase their percentage but still fall well below the target (Austria, Japan, Switzerland, and the United Kingdom). The contribution from the United States, which accounts for roughly half of the total GNP of such countries, continues to decline. It has already fallen from above .5 per cent of GNP in the early years of the last decade to .31 per cent in 1970. It is likely to fall further to around .24 per cent by 1975.

I feel obliged, therefore, to conclude that the total flows of ODA for the first half of the decade are likely to average out at approximately .37 per cent of GNP, only half of the Second Development Decade target.

This is a most unwelcome conclusion, but we must face facts. Not only is there no evidence that ODA as a percentage of GNP will rise above one-half of the target rate by 1975, but unless there are prompt and marked changes in attitudes, it is difficult to foresee any great improvement in the second half of the decade.

Was the .7 per cent target too ambitious? Are the difficulties within the domestic economies of the developed countries such that it is unrealistic to assume they can afford this degree of assistance to international development?

Certainly not.

During the First Development Decade, the total GNP of

---

ments made by governments. Because of the relatively long periods of time required to translate legislative authorizations first into commitments and later into disbursements, it is possible to project today, with reasonable accuracy, ODA flows (which by definition represent disbursements) for 1975.

the world increased by $1,100 billion. That is an increase in income almost beyond comprehension. But how was that growth in income distributed throughout the world? Eighty per cent of the increase went to countries where per capita incomes already average over $1,000—and they contain only one-quarter of the world's population. Only 6 per cent of the increase went to countries where per capita incomes average $200 or less—but they contain 60 per cent of the world's people.

Today the average per capita income in the developed countries is approximately $2,400. The comparable figure for the developing countries is $180. By 1980, after the one-quarter of the world's people who live in the developed countries once again receive 80 per cent of the total increase in the world's income, their per capita income will have risen by some $1,200. The comparable increase in the per capita income of the three-quarters of the world's people who live in the developing countries—even if the Second Development Decade growth objective is achieved—will be less than $100.

The collective GNP of the developed countries in 1970 totaled roughly $2,000 billion. In constant prices, it is projected to grow to at least $3,000 billion by 1980. What this means is that in order to raise the current ODA flows of .35 per cent to the targeted .7 per cent, the developed countries would need to devote only about 1.5 per cent of the amount by which they themselves will grow richer during the decade. The remaining 98.5 per cent of their incremental income will provide them with sufficient funds to meet their domestic priorities.

Granted these facts, are we to say seriously that these wealthy countries cannot reach the ODA target of .7 per cent of their combined GNP's? It is manifestly not a case of their being unable to afford it. Nor, in my view, is the serious shortfall in Official Development Assistance due to the lack of generosity of the peoples of the developed world or their indifference.

It is more a matter of ignorance—a failure to comprehend the inhuman conditions that characterize the lives of hundreds of millions of people in the developing countries, a failure to grasp how severe the maldistribution of income actually is between rich nations and poor nations, and a failure to understand how modest are the amounts of the wealthy nations' incremental income which, if made available to the developing countries, would make so great a difference in their ability to meet minimal growth objectives.

It is said that in wealthy countries the case for foreign assistance has no constituency. I do not believe that is true. What I do believe is that the constituency in most of the countries must be better informed, better mobilized, and better motivated. In the end, that is a matter of leadership. But if that constituency in important parts of the developed world remains at its present low level of concern—and governments continue to reflect this—then one is compelled to conclude that the flow of Official Development Assistance will remain at its present wholly inadequate level throughout the decade.

In view of the degree of poverty that oppresses the human spirit, in so much of the world, that would be tragic. Let me, for a moment, analyze what in fact that failure would mean.

The ODA deficit will penalize the poorest countries the most. It is unlikely that they will be able to reach the growth target. Their need for ODA is the greatest, and if it stagnates at its present level, they will feel the effects the most severely. But, for even those developing countries that are somewhat better off, a deficiency in ODA will force them to seek external finance from less desirable sources, particularly those demanding high rates of interest or early repayment. The danger of overreliance on such sources is well known: it adds significantly to short- and medium-term debt burdens by mortgaging larger proportions of export earnings, and, in the event of an unexpected decline in those earnings, it can cause severe strains on the whole of the economy.

The truth is that if ODA flows level off at substantially less than the target for the decade, mounting debt problems for the developing world are inevitable. In the face of an ODA deficit, the developing countries would either have to reduce their rates of growth or increase their debts above reasonable levels. They are likely to do both.

Since the mid-1950's, publicly guaranteed debt has been growing at about 14 per cent a year. At the end of 1972 it stood at about $75 billion, and annual debt service exceeded $7 billion. Servicing of debt rose by 18 per cent in 1970 and by 20 per cent in 1971. The average rate of increase since the 1960's has been about twice the rate at which export earnings, from which debt must be serviced, have been growing. Such a relationship cannot continue indefinitely.

With the prospect of a leveling off of Official Development Assistance at far less than the targeted amount and its partial replacement with financial assistance on harder terms, debt-service ratios will inevitably rise. Debt financing has a continuing role in development, but it has its outer limits of prudence and these must be recognized by debtors and creditors alike.

If the developing countries are to offset shortfalls in ODA and keep debt burdens within manageable proportions, it is clear that their most imperative need is greatly to expand their export earnings. How can this be done? Can it be done at all?

It can. But only by difficult economic adjustments, broad

policy changes, and astute political leadership in the rich
and poor countries alike. The general outline of the problem
is clear enough. From an export point of view, there are three
broad categories of developing countries:

- Those countries that export fuel. Fuel exports account for a
third of all export earnings in the developing world, and are
growing at an average rate of 10 per cent a year. But three-
quarters of these substantial earnings go to only six countries,
containing less than 3 per cent of the world's population.

- Those countries, many of them with very low income, that
remain highly dependent on exports of agricultural products.

- Those countries, many of them in the middle-income group,
in which it is possible to increase earnings through exports of
manufactures.

The relative inelasticity of demand for agricultural raw
materials means that the growth of exports of primary commodities, excluding fuel and minerals, is not likely to exceed
3 or 4 per cent a year. However, even for countries dependent
on the exports of such products, the developed countries
can provide assistance.

They can negotiate stabilization agreements—on the international coffee agreement model—for cocoa and other commodities. Such agreements might provide for multilateral
financial assistance, and the wealthier nations could well
afford to leave more of their markets open to agricultural
imports from developing countries. Agricultural protection-
ism, particularly in the current climate of inflationary food
prices in wealthy nations, makes neither domestic nor international sense. The sugar beet growers of the temperate
countries, for example, have other ways of earning their
living; the sugarcane growers of the Caribbean, Mauritius,
and Fiji do not, and the same could be said for many other
commodities.

For the developing countries with greater capabilities for the export of manufactures—countries whose populations total over one billion—we have estimated that achievement of the 6 per cent growth target will require an increase in their export earnings, in current prices, of nearly 10 per cent a year. This, in turn, necessitates an annual increase of their manufactured exports of 15 per cent.

Can this be achieved?

It is necessary to look back over the industrial strategy of the developing countries in the past two decades to gain even a tentative answer to that question. Postwar industrial expansion in the developing world has been very impressive. In most developing countries manufacturing has been the fastest growing sector, although starting from a very small base. Manufacturing in the developing world increased at an average rate of 6 to 7 per cent between 1950 and 1970, exceeding the rate of increase in most of the industrial nations of today at a comparable stage of their development. Manufacturing now accounts for 17 per cent of the combined gross domestic product of developing countries, as compared to 12 per cent two decades earlier. Its contribution to employment creation, however, was limited. With annual increases of about 4 per cent, manufacturing employment absorbed less than one-fifth of the approximately 200 million increase in the labor force between 1950 and 1970.

In a very real sense the contribution that manufacturing makes to economic development is understated if its contribution is based only on the value of its output or on the number of jobs it provides. For countries whose economies are dependent on the export of a few primary products, perhaps with poor long-run prospects of fluctuating prices, it contributes an important degree of diversification. Industrialization furthers the training of a skilled labor force. It encourages the emergence of managers and indigenous entrepreneurs and expands the development of a local capital market. It also tends to promote investment in infrastructure and technical facilities that might not otherwise be economically feasible. In other words, it contributes to modernization in general.

The desirability of expanding the industrial sector has therefore been obvious for many years to the governments of most developing nations. When starting the process, those with sizable internal markets have naturally begun by producing at home items which they have had to import in the past.* Usually these are simple consumer goods. In order to encourage domestic production, protective policies against imports, such as high import duties or quota restrictions, have often been applied.

It is hard to think of any other way in which the industrialization process could get started. But once the process is under way, developing countries are confronted with an important choice that substantially affects the benefits they can derive from industrialization. This choice is whether to continue to rely on the domestic market as the basis for industrial expansion or to attempt to break out into foreign markets. At this point many, if not most, of the developing countries have made the wrong choice. They have continued too far along the path of import substitution.

Experience has shown that, though this pattern of industrialization may for some years be conducive to high growth rates of manufacturing output, sooner or later it faces increasing difficulties. In the first place, once imports of any product have been replaced, that industry's growth is limited to the growth of the domestic market. To maintain industrial momentum requires import substitution in continually new

---

* In small countries (and most of the developing countries are small) the possibilities of pursuing an import-substitution strategy are limited by extremely small domestic markets.

products. Frequently this means moving into products less and less suited to the size of the market and the nature of the economy. Many developing countries—already short of capital, and burdened with high unemployment—have found themselves in the uneconomic position of providing high levels of protection to capital-intensive industries.

There are other difficulties as well. High levels of protection have often made it possible to maintain overvalued exchange rates. This has penalized exports, and, since most capital goods are imported, has kept the price of capital equipment low, thereby encouraging the uneconomical use of labor-saving techniques.

These problems can be overcome by an alternative strategy of development that gives greater emphasis to manufacture for export. The industries stimulated by such a program will be those most suited to conditions in developing countries. Many are likely to be relatively labor-intensive, thus contributing to the solution of the employment problem. Production for foreign as well as domestic markets should help ensure the benefits of large-scale production.

These advantages are not merely hypothetical. The results in countries which have oriented their manufacturing sectors toward exporting have been more promising than those in countries relying entirely on import substitution. Their industrial growth rates—often as much as 10 to 15 per cent—have been higher, and the expansion of employment has been substantially faster.

Undoubtedly it is easier to shift to greater exporting before the structure of manufacturing becomes fixed in a distorted high-cost pattern. Recent achievements in Mexico, Brazil,* and Yugoslavia, however, suggest that it is possible for

* By reorienting its industrial sector from import substitution to exports, Brazil increased its export earnings from manufactured goods from $144 million to $412 million in only four years' time (1966–70).

countries which have long emphasized import substitution to adjust export incentives to offset protection and, as a result, to enjoy a marked increase in manufactured exports.

Policies outside the foreign trade field also are important in determining the pattern of manufacturing development and labor absorption. All too often investment in capital goods in the developing countries has been encouraged by tax concessions and subsidized interest rates, while use of labor has been discouraged by revenue systems based primarily on payroll taxes. Such taxes are extraordinarily high in many countries of Latin America. In one, for example, they amount to 28 per cent of the wage paid. There is no reason why education, pensions, insurance, housing, and the many other public expenditures for which these taxes are used should not be financed in a way that has a less harmful effect on the volume of employment.

There is no conflict here between employment creation and economic growth. Industrial policies that cause prices to reflect more accurately the scarcity of capital and the abundance of labor will lead not only to greater output and a healthier balance of payments but to increased employment as well.

The suggestion that developing countries base their trade and industrial policies on a clear recognition of international opportunities and of the relative scarcities of productive factors has been made many times. Yet the subject is often received with a good deal of skepticism. It is worth discussing why.

In the first place, it is sometimes doubted whether an appropriate labor-intensive technology exists in most branches of manufacturing industry. I agree that the choice of technology is often limited, and certainly a good many of the apparently more labor-intensive methods of production are inefficient and obsolete. Nevertheless, there is evidence that in the production of many products it is very possible to substitute labor for capital. This is particularly true in the transport, handling, and packaging of materials. There are also possibilities for more widespread use of the multiple-shift operations.

There are a number of examples where differences in the relative costs of labor and capital have led to new techniques of production. In the case, for instance, of the production of plywood in Korea, what 'at first appears to be a manufacturing process very similar to that carried out in the United States turns out on inspection to be full of innovative and indigenous variations. In America, mechanical sensors are used to detect defects in pieces of timber, and the entire slab is then discarded. In Japan, defects are located and then cut out by hand. In Korea, the defective area—a knothole, for example—is located and patched up by hand.

Admittedly, the empirical knowledge in all these matters is incomplete. That is why the Bank is at present exploring ways in which it might encourage the development of more labor-intensive technologies and why our research program is examining the possibilties of labor/capital substitution, in order to provide both ourselves and our member countries with a more complete picture of how these issues work out in practice.

An even more critical question to this general line of reasoning is whether, if developing countries produce manufactured goods at competitive prices, the tendency of advanced nations to protect their existing industries will block their export.

Growth in exports of manufactured goods from the developing to the developed countries has already been rapid. They increased at an annual rate of about 15 per cent during the period 1962–69. They started, however, from such a small base that the share of the manufactured exports of the developing countries remains only 5 per cent of the manufactured imports of the developed nations, and one-third of 1 per cent of their GNP.

If manufactured imports from the developing nations could continue to grow at 15 per cent until 1980—and if aid targets are met—this would be enough to offset the slow growth of primary exports and to satisfy projected import requirements.

But a 15 per cent rate of growth in manufactured exports will be harder to achieve in the 1970's than it was in the 1960's. To do so, annual exports, which rose from less than $2 billion in 1960 to $7 billion in 1970, will have to quadruple to $28 billion in 1980. Even if this level were to be reached by 1980, the total volume of such exports would still remain a very small part—approximately 7 per cent—of the expected manufactured imports of the advanced countries, and only 1 per cent of their projected GNP.

Although these exports need not all be aimed exclusively at the markets of the richer countries, the principal markets must be provided in the developed nations. The developing countries have justifiable grounds for complaining that they are being treated unfairly in their attempts to expand their manufactured exports to those markets. On the average, tariffs are higher on the kinds of manufactured goods imported from poor countries than on imports from rich countries. According to a recent study, tariffs on the two groups of imports average 7 and 12 per cent in the United States, 9 and 14′ per cent in the United Kingdom, and 7 and 9 per cent in the European Community.

Even worse than the absolute level of tariffs is their structure. Tariffs rise with the degree of fabrication. Thus, in the European Community cocoa beans imported from non-associated countries bear a 3 per cent duty, while the tariff on processed cocoa products is 18 per cent. In the United States, hides and skins enter duty-free, but tariffs of 4 to 5 per cent apply on leather and 8 to 10 per cent on shoes. This margin could well offset the comparative advantages in processing found in many developing countries.

Finally, and perhaps worst of all, nontariff barriers to trade have proliferated throughout the rich countries in recent years. Restrictions on market access exist in a variety of administrative and fiscal measures, including quotas, subsidies, valuation techniques, and preferential buying arrangements under government procurement. These, too, are more severe for developing countries.

An important element of the U.N. development strategy for the 1970's is the proposal that the developed countries grant preferential treatment to the manufactured exports of developing countries. Representatives of eighteen industrialized countries have undertaken to try to implement this proposal. The European Community, the Nordic countries, and Japan have already adopted the plan, with various limitations. However, even if all eighteen countries comply, these measures will enable the developing nations to increase their trade by only $1 billion a year.* If the remaining $20 billion of additional exports per year is to be achieved during the 1970's, the developing countries must radically change their industrial policy from import substitution to export-oriented manufacturing, and the developed countries must provide the necessary markets by greater efforts to remove discriminatory trade restrictions.

We must face the fact that expanding the volume of manufactured imports from the poor countries into the rich countries, while benefiting the majority of the citizens of the rich countries, will involve injuries to certain sectors of their

* Over a three- to five-year period, approximately $400 million annually would be represented by additional imports into the European Economic Community; $400 million, by additional imports into the United States; and $200 million, by additional imports into other developed countries.

economies. These injuries will be strongly resisted—and rightly so—by the individuals and firms affected, unless appropriate adjustment assistance policies and procedures fully in step with the reduction of tariff and nontariff barriers are introduced. Few developed countries now possess such policies and procedures.

To urge both the developed countries and the developing countries to expand their trade with one another—the former by more freely admitting labor-intensive imports, and the latter by not resorting to excessive import substitution—is not to urge that one set of countries do the other set of countries a favor. I am simply recommending that each recognize where their true mutual interests lie.

5

Affluence, the Environment, and Development

As the enormity of the population explosion begins to be understood by the public in the developed world, some doubts have arisen about the possibility of improving the lot of so many billions of people. Do the rich countries have the capacity to help the poorer countries to develop themselves? And if they do, does the earth's biosphere contain the resources needed to provide a decent life for all its new billions of inhabitants?

I touched briefly on the problem of whether the rich can afford to help the poor in Chapter 4, and I should like to expand on the point now. The argument is often made, particularly in the United States, that rich countries must at least first take care of their own poor before they worry about the poor of other nations. Charity, we are reminded, begins at home.

I suggest that this argument, while appealing, misses the point. For instance, the President of the United States has pointed out that in this decade the U.S. will increase its wealth by 50 per cent and that the gross national product in 1979, at constant prices, will be $500 billion greater than in 1969. The fact is, then, that the American economy is so immense it can readily support a just and reasonable foreign aid program of the general dimensions outlined by the report of the Pearson Commission on International Development and at the same time deal justly and effectively with domestic needs. The country is clearly wealthy enough to do so.

There is no lack of capacity in the American economy to meet this twofold responsibility. What may be lacking is a broad commitment of the national will to do so. Or perhaps the lack is not so much one of national will as a lack of national understanding—or not so much a case of indifference to responsibility as a case of understandable confusion over the competing claims on attention and national resolve.

What is certainly true is that the decision to respond both to pressures of domestic problems and to the urgency of essential foreign assistance is, in the end, dependent on the response to a far more basic and searching question—a question that must be faced not in the United States alone but in every wealthy, industrialized country of the world. That question is this: Which is ultimately more in a nation's interest—to funnel national resources into an endlessly spiraling consumer economy (in effect, a pursuit of consumer gadgetry with all its by-products of waste and pollution) or to dedicate a more reasonable share of those same sources to improving the fundamental quality of life both at home and abroad?

The dilemma that faces the wealthy nations of the world is not whether they should devote more of their gross national product to solving domestic crises and less of it to helping eliminate inhuman deprivations abroad, but rather whether they are going to seek a more equitable balance between private opulence and public responsibility. Private wealth cannot be preserved and public responsibility cannot be met by a heedless indifference to common crises that in the end will touch rich and poor alike.

What we must grasp is that gross measures of economic strength and growth—for example, levels of GNP and rates of change of GNP—as necessary as they are, cannot measure the soundness of the social structure of a nation. The United States itself is a classic illustration of this truth. Technologically the most advanced society on earth, it produces the greatest GNP ever recorded in history and enjoys a per capita income that is thirty times greater than that of the peoples in a quarter of the nations of the world.

But what do such figures mean when we remember that, even for the affluent, life is beset by smog, pollution, noise, traffic congestion, urban violence, youthful disaffection, and a terrifying increase in the drug problem? Worse still, the wealthiest society on earth includes more than 25 million people so poor that their lives verge on mere subsistence. In 1971, 9 per cent of all white families and 29 per cent of all black families in the United States subsisted beneath the poverty line.

The poor in America are like the poor everywhere. Statistically their economic condition is improving, but the progress is so slow in relation to the more advantaged groups in society that they are actually growing poorer relative to the rich. The point is illustrative of a phenomenon common throughout the world. Though men have inhabited the same planet for more than a million years, they coexist today in communities whose extremes range from stone-age simplicity to space-age sophistication.

That degree of inequality would not, perhaps, be as socially and politically explosive as it in fact is, could it remain a well-kept secret. For centuries stagnating societies and deprived peoples remained content with their lot because they were unaware that life was really any better elsewhere. Their very remoteness saved them from odious comparisons. The technological revolution changed all that. Today, the transistor radio and the television tube in remote corners of the world dramatize the disparities in the equality of life. What was tolerable in the past provokes turbulence today.

What else but turbulence could one expect on a planet linked by instantaneous communication but fragmented by conspicuous inequality? It is inconceivable that one-quarter of mankind, moving forward into a self-accelerating affluence, can succeed in walling itself off from the other three-quarters, who find themselves entrapped in a self-perpetuating cycle of poverty.

The outlook for this decade is that the fault line along which shocks to world stability travel will shift from an east-west axis to a north-south axis, and the shocks themselves will be significantly less military in character and substantially more political, social, and economic.

In view of this, it is tragic and senseless that the world is spending $183 billion a year [in 1970] on armaments—a sum twenty-four times larger than the total spent in all foreign assistance programs. What is even worse is that defense spending is increasing by some 6 per cent a year, a growth rate in destructive power that is greater than the growth rate of the world's total production of all goods and services. And the final irony in this litany of irrationalities is that arms spending in the developing countries is increasing at the rate of 7.5 per cent a year against the world average of 6 per cent.

The blunt truth is that the state of development in most of the developing world today is unacceptable. It is unacceptable, but not because there has not been progress. There has been. The total economic growth, measured in GNP terms, for the developing countries during the First Development Decade was impressive. For some of these countries it was the most successful decade in their history when measured in these gross economic terms.

Such economic measurements, however—useful as they are —can be seriously inadequate. They do not in themselves tell us much about what is happening to the great masses of people in the developing countries, hundreds of millions of whose lives are not being touched significantly by development. There are two overriding reasons for this: The developing countries are not moving decisively enough to reduce the severe social and economic inequities among their own peoples (a subject I will discuss in the next chapter), and the developed countries are not moving decisively enough to reduce the gross imbalance between their own opulence and the penury of the less privileged nations. Development simply cannot succeed unless that massively distorted distribution of income—at both national and international levels—is brought into a more just and reasonable balance. Action is required by rich nations and poor, and that action can only proceed in a climate of growth.

It is here that the complexity of the problem becomes apparent. For a poor country to operate an economy that distributes income among the people more justly, there manifestly must be economic growth. Without economic growth a poor country will remain poor. There is little point in trying to redistribute indigence. But economic growth means manipulating the traditional environment. As we now know well enough, it is at this point that injury to the environment can take place. If nature is abused beyond limits, its revenge is inevitable.

The poor nations are faced with the problem of growth within acceptable environmental limits, but the rich nations are faced with the same dilemma and to an even greater extent, for the evidence is overwhelming that a century of rapid economic expansion has contributed to a cumulatively monstrous assault on the quality of life in the developed countries. The horns of the dilemma are these: The achievement of a level of life in accord with fundamental human dignity for the world's more than two billion poor is simply not possible without the continued economic growth of the developing nations and the developed nations as well. But economic growth on the pattern of the past—and most particularly that in the already highly industrialized wealthy nations—poses an undeniable threat to the environment and to the health of man.

There is nothing artificial or contrived about the dilemma. It is very real. Both its elements demand the most deliberate attention. The question is not whether there should be continued economic growth. There must be. Nor is the question whether the impact on the environment must be respected. It has to be. Nor, least of all, is it a question of whether these two considerations are interlocked. They are. The solution of the dilemma depends not on whether but on how.

At its macro level, this dilemma demands a great deal more research than it has yet received, not merely to provide us with a better understanding of the over-all resolution of the dilemma, but to amend in a more scholarly manner the alarmist views of some who are deeply persuaded of the problem but unaware of the complexity of its elements. Mathematical modeling is useful, but only as useful as the validity of its assumptions and the comprehensiveness of its inputs.

What is needed in this issue—and has not yet been achieved —is the close cooperation of economists and ecologists, of social and physical scientists, of experienced political leaders and development project specialists. The manifest danger in the solution of this dilemma at the macro level is oversimplification.

When that oversimplification suggests the imminent risk

of overloading the planet's life-support systems or exhausting its essential resources, the developing peoples of the world are suddenly faced with a fearsome prospect. On top of all their present disadvantages, are they now going to be asked to forgo their efforts at development in the name of preserving the already disproportionate (and still rising) patterns of consumption of the rich?

The poor are right to be indignant over such a prospect, but in my view that issue need never arise, because there is no evidence that the economic growth the developing countries so desperately require will necessarily involve an unacceptable burden either on their own or on anybody else's environment. Let me illustrate this view by a brief account of what we in the World Bank are doing to deal with the environmental issue in our day-to-day operations.

In 1970 we established the post of Environmental Advisor with a strong mandate to review and evaluate every investment project from the standpoint of its potential effects on the environment. Our subsequent experience has been that the most careful review of environmental issues need not handicap our fundamental task of furthering the progress of development. On the contrary, it can enhance and accelerate that progress.

In cooperation with other development agencies, we have designed a careful set of guidelines and have built into our whole economic assistance strategy a feasible method for correlating ecological protection with effective and cost-conscious development. We have made a significant discovery in the process. By careful analysis, we have found in every instance to date that we can reduce the danger of environmental hazards either at no cost to the project or at a cost so moderate that the borrower has readily agreed to accept the necessary safeguards.

Central to the success of this approach is the principle that, in the issue of environmental damage, prevention is infinitely preferable to cure. Not only is it more effective, it is clearly less expensive. Responsible officials in the developing countries are aware of this. We in the Bank have found no evidence that they are unresponsive to what can be demonstrated to be a serious ecological hazard or a threat to health and social well-being. It is unfair to suggest that the poor countries are indifferent to the environmental issue or that they dismiss it out of hand as a rich nation's problem. They do not. What they are justifiably concerned about is that some of the rich nations, under the influence of doomsday alarmism, may be tempted to set up unilateral and unreasonable roadblocks in the way of poor countries' desperate efforts to develop. The poor nations have no desire to see their own environment contaminated or wantonly abused, but neither do they want to remain trapped as victims of the permanent contamination of poverty.

Our experience is that environmental protection can be built into development projects as competently and successfully as any other requisite element. Our project officers are thoroughly briefed on our environmental guidelines and bring these to the attention of potential borrowers at an early stage of the discussions. Far from being resented, this approach is welcomed.

Each project processed in the Bank is now reviewed by the Environmental Office, and a careful in-house study is made of the ecological components. If the project warrants it, an on-site "ecological reconnaissance" study is commissioned by the Bank with the use of qualified consultants. If more serious problems are uncovered, a still more intensive on-site evaluation is undertaken in order to determine what specialized solutions should be incorporated into the project's specifications.

While in principle the Bank could refuse a loan on environmental grounds—in a situation, for example, in which the problems are of such severity that adequate safeguards cannot be applied, or in which the borrower is wholly unwilling to take reasonable measures in his own interest— the fact is that no such case has yet arisen. Since initiating our environmental review, we have found that in every instance the recommended safeguards can and have been successfully negotiated and implemented.

We have been careful to base our environmental guidelines not merely on physical and health-related factors but on cultural considerations as well. We in the Bank are concerned that a development project does not adversely affect the indigenous culture that the country wishes to preserve. When a project requires the relocation of people, we make sure that plans are adequate for their successful resettlement and that injurious disruptions of their socio-economic opportunities are avoided.

Health factors are, of course, often involved in environmental considerations. In those instances where a development project may threaten to create a new (or intensify an existing) disease problem, the Bank incorporates in the loan agreement appropriate arrangements for the requisite preventive health care measures.

The Bank does not limit its operations to the environmental side effects of development projects. It finances many projects with specific environmental goals—urban water supply and sewage treatment, for example, as well as soil erosion control and water resources management. The environmental criteria we have established in the Bank encompass the entire spectrum of development. They consist of a comprehensive checklist of questions designed to ensure that foreseeable and injurious environmental consequences are carefully considered from the conception of a project, through its design stage and actual construction, and into its ongoing operations.

The checklist includes sectors as diverse as textiles and tourism, power stations and paper plants, steel-making and irrigation systems, fertilizer factories and harbor facilities—and many, many more. Sample questions in a few of these sectors illustrate their range and scope:

Irrigation Systems. Will the changes in water patterns introduce disease-bearing organisms into previously unaffected areas? Will runoff water contain residues—such as pesticides and fertilizers—that contaminate downstream waters? Will there be sedimentation and erosion problems? What will be the ecological consequences of changes in land patterns and population distribution?

Ports and Harbor Development. Will topographical changes adversely affect marine life? How will wave and current action be modified? Will ships create unhealthy air pollution from stacks in view of prevailing winds? Will the development create waterfront slum areas?

Fertilizer Plants. What types and quantities of gaseous, liquid, and solid effluents will be discharged into the air, soil and water? Will nitrogen and phosphorous entering surface water bodies stimulate the growth of algae and aquatic weeds? How will raw materials be handled and stored?

Petrochemical Complexes. Have hydrologic, geologic, seismologic, and meteorologic studies of the site been made to anticipate and minimize damage to human populations and the environment if accidents occur? Will effluents contain toxic materials? How will they be controlled? What are the dangers of oil or chemical spills? What clean-up contingency plans are available?

Highway Construction. Do plans include provisions for preventing unnecessary despoilment of the landscape and vegetation during construction? Will topsoil be stored for respreading? Can temporary drainage systems, barriers, and sedimentation basins be used to prevent eroding materials from reaching waterways? Have provisions been made for adequate living conditions for people displaced by construction activities or for those attracted to newly opened areas?

These are merely examples of the kinds of issues raised. The full checklist is far more comprehensive, and it provides borrowers with precisely the questions they themselves should consider in their planning for pragmatic environmental protection. The projects that pass for review through our Environmental Office are concerned with every major region of the developing world. Here are a few case histories by way of example:

● In its funding of the expansion of a steel plant in Turkey on the Black Sea, the Bank cooperated with the borrower in building into the specifications—as a result of thorough on-site study—provisions to control within acceptable levels the flow of liquid wastes into the sea and gaseous effluents into the air. Originally no such controls had been contemplated. The study convinced the borrower that this would result in unacceptable damage to both offshore waters and the surrounding terrain, and the recommended pollution-control technology was adopted. The cost for providing this important protection for the environment, as well as for the health of the local population, was only 2 per cent of the over-all project costs.

● In the Yagoua district of Cameroon, the rice farmers are poor. The Bank's estimate was that their cash income could increase fivefold in a decade if only irrigation facilities could be improved. But a serious environmental hazard had to be reckoned with: bilharzia. This water-borne disease is carried by the Bulinas snail and is endemic to the area. Though the proposed irrigation network would serve 3,000 hectares of land and 2,800 farm families, it was feared that the project might significantly increase the incidence of illness. To assess the problem, the Bank sent a highly qualified expert in the control of the snail vector to Cameroon. After on-site research, his report recommended changes in the engineering design of the canals, provisions for periodic surveys of the snail population, and appropriate molluscicide application as required. The borrower welcomed these recommendations, adopted them, and during the loan negotiations further agreed that public health officials would carefully monitor the region. Thus, an urgent development project was protected from potential ecological risk by inexpensive and practical preventive measures.

• In its financing of a marine terminal at Sepetiba Bay in Brazil --as part of an iron ore mining project near Belo Horizonte and its attendant rail transportation to the sea—the Bank commissioned an ecological team to study in depth what was required to keep this unspoiled estuary free from pollution. The bay supported an important fishing industry and possessed tourist and recreational potential. The Bank's team included a marine biologist, a shellfish expert, and an oceanographer. Their recommendations have been built into the loan agreement and provide for protection against ore and oil carriers flushing their huge holds in the bay, contingency equipment for accidental oil spills, solid waste handling and terminal sewage treatment facilities, and landscaping to preserve the aesthetic values of the area. All of these measures—which will ensure that the fishing industry can survive and the bay remain a tourist and recreational attraction—represent less than 3 per cent of the total project cost.

These case histories can be multiplied many times, but what is common to them all is that they illustrate a critical truth: Valid environmental considerations need not deny the advance in economic development that the less privileged countries so gravely require.

In environmental matters the developing countries enjoy one of the very few advantages of being latecomers in the development process—they are in a position to avoid some of the more costly and needless mistakes the developed countries have made in the past. Now what does that imply?

To begin with, what it does *not* imply is that latecomers to the development process must forgo industrialization and technological advance. That would mean stagnation. It is easy enough for the wealthy to romanticize about the supposed charm of pretechnological society. The plain fact is that there was nothing pretty at all about the squalid poverty that the common man had to endure in the pretechnological period in what are now the affluent nations. For the vast majority it was a life of destitution and disease. No one wants to go back to that. Anyone in doubt has only to examine poverty in the developing countries today. The deprivation is appalling by any acceptable standards of human decency. It is not surprising, then, that those who call for a slowing down or a complete halt to economic growth tend to be those who are already amply provided with the advantages made possible by that very growth.

What the "environmental advantage of latecomers to the development process" *does* imply is that they can far more easily and inexpensively build into their industrial infrastructure the practical preventive measures necessary to avoid the ecological damage the developed world has already suffered.

Our experience in the Bank confirms this. There is an increasingly broad variety of antipollution technologies available to the poorer countries—technologies the affluent countries have had to develop at a far later and more difficult stage of their industrial expansion.

Those technologies can work, and work well. The air over London is substantially cleaner today than it was fifteen years ago. There has been an 80 per cent reduction in smoke emission in that city, a 40 per cent reduction in sulphur dioxide, and a consequent near doubling in the average hours of winter sunshine. It is estimated that this dramatic improvement—largely the result of the enlightened Clean Air Act of 1956—has cost Londoners only about 40 cents per capita per annum. What it has saved them in discomfort and illness is beyond calculation, but one need only recall the disastrous and fatal smog of 1952, which killed an estimated 4,000 Londoners, to appreciate the importance of the improvement.

There has been a corresponding improvement in the environmental conditions of many of the rivers in Britain through intensified sewage management. Ten years ago there were no fish at all in the Thames in a thirty-mile stretch above and below the city of London. Three years ago more than forty species were observed in the same stretch.

As the affluent nations continue to take their environmental problems more seriously, they are going to discover a whole new range of technology to abate and avoid ecological dangers. The less privileged countries can adapt these technical advances to their own local conditions.

The danger that we will fail to achieve our twin objectives of advancing the development of the less privileged nations and at the same time preserving their environment stems not from a lack of the necessary technology but from a lack of political will and social responsibility.

Ecological considerations have made us all more aware of the interdependence of the political and geographical entities of our world. We have come to see our planet as a single entity, the "spaceship earth." But what we must not forget is that one-quarter of the passengers on that ship have luxurious first-class accommodations and the remaining three-quarters are traveling in steerage. That does not make for a happy ship—in space or anywhere else. All the less so when the steerage passengers realize that the means are at hand to make the accommodations reasonably comfortable for everyone.

Have we the political and social awareness to give more attention to the present living conditions of the overwhelming majority of the travelers? That would mean, in practice, making available more development assistance and removing inequitable trade, tariff, and other discriminatory barriers. As I have stated in earlier chapters, the suggestion that the rich countries cannot spare for the poor countries the miniscule percentage of that incremental income necessary to raise concessionary aid from its present level of .35 per cent of GNP to the United Nations target of .7 per cent is beyond credence.

The wealthy nations may not in fact meet that target. They may delay dismantling the discriminatory barriers holding back a more just and mutually advantageous flow of trade. But if the rich do refuse greater trade and aid to the poor, it will have nothing to do with a disinterested and universal reverence for the environment. It will be because of a provincial response to the pressures of special interests.

What then, must be done to reconcile our mandate to assist in the economic advance of the developing countries with our responsibility to preserve and enhance the environment? In my view, five essential requirements must be met. We must:

1. Recognize that economic growth in the developing countries is essential if they are to deal with their human problems;

2. Act on the evidence that such growth, if properly planned, need not result in unacceptable ecological penalties;

3. Assist the developing countries in their choice of a pattern of growth that will yield a combination of high economic gain with low environmental risk;

4. Provide the external support required for that economic advance by moving more rapidly toward meeting the United Nations concessionary aid target of .7 per cent of the gross national product, and by dismantling and discarding inequitable trade barriers that restrict exports from poorer countries; and

5. Above all, realize that human degradation is the most dangerous pollutant there is.

6

Social Equity and Economic Growth

G iven the unfortunate shortfall in aid, the consequent
aggravation of the debt problem, and the procrastination of the developed countries in dismantling discriminatory
barriers to trade from the developing countries, the Second
Development Decade's 6 per cent growth target is not going
to be met by many nations and represents an exceptionally
arduous task for many others. But let us suppose that it were
in fact to be accomplished by 1980. Would that achievement,
in itself, guarantee a significant advance in the quality of
life for the majority of the two billion people who live in our
developing member countries?

The frank answer is no—because increases in national income, as essential as they are, will not benefit the poor unless
they reach the poor. They have not reached the poor to any
significant degree in most developing countries in the past,

in spite of historically unprecedented average rates of growth throughout the 1960's.

In the last decade, for example, Brazil's gross national product per capita in real terms grew by 2.5 per cent per year. Yet the share of the national income received by the poorest 40 per cent of the population declined from 10 per cent in 1960 to 8 per cent in 1970, whereas the share of the richest 5 per cent grew from 29 per cent to 38 per cent during the same period. In GNP terms, the country did well. The very rich did very well. But throughout the decade the benefit to the poorest 40 per cent of the population was only marginal.

In Mexico the picture is similar. Between 1950 and 1969 the average income per capita grew, in real terms, by 3 per cent per year. The richest 10 per cent of the population received about half of the total national income at the beginning of the period and an even larger share at the end of the period (49 per cent and 51 per cent). But the share of the poorest 40 per cent of the people, only 14 per cent in 1950, declined to 11 per cent in 1969. The share of the poorest 20 per cent during the same period sank from 6 per cent to 4 per cent.

In India, there has been progress in over-all GNP growth during the past decade. But today some 40 per cent of the entire population—200 million people—live at a level below the poverty line, a level at which serious malnutrition begins. The poorest 10 per cent of the nation—50 million people— have not only not shared in the progress of the decade but may even have grown poorer.

These examples are not atypical. A recent study of income distribution patterns in more than forty developing countries estimates that at the beginning of the First Development Decade the average share in the national income of the richest 20 per cent of the people was 56 per cent, whereas the share of the poorest 60 per cent of the people was only 26 per cent. Although comparable data for the beginning of the Second Development Decade are as yet too sketchy for us to draw detailed conclusions, preliminary indications are that this severely distorted income distribution is not only continuing but in many countries may be growing worse. The poor are sharing only to a very limited extent in the benefits of growth.

To understand this fully it is necessary to distinguish three broad categories of poverty in the developing world. First, there is great poverty in those generally rather small countries that have very few resources—natural, financial, or skilled—with which to promote growth. There is so little wealth in these nations that even if it were more equitably distributed, virtually everyone would still be very poor. There are twenty-five such countries, with populations totaling 140 million. The United Nations has designated these the least developed countries, and special measures of assistance for them have been approved.

Second, there is the poverty found in certain impoverished regions in most of the larger developing countries—for example, the southern republics of Yugoslavia, northeastern Brazil, and northeastern Thailand. The integration of these regions into the more rapidly growing parts of the economy often poses difficult cultural as well as economic problems. These areas are, however, readily identifiable geographically, and it is possible to devise and implement programs for increasing the productive capacities and incomes of their populations, based on the geographical features of the regions.

The third category of poverty is the most extensive, the most pervasive, and the most persistent of all. It is the poverty of the low-income strata—roughly the poorest 40 per cent of the total population in all developing countries. It is they who, despite their country's gross economic growth, remain trapped in conditions of deprivation that fall below any rational definition of human decency.

This is not simply the poverty of a highly disadvantaged country, or of a particularly backward geographical region in an otherwise rapidly advancing country. Rather, it is the poverty of those people widely dispersed throughout every developing country who, for whatever reason, lie beyond the reach of market forces and existing public services. It is the poverty of those masses of the population that current government policies do not adequately encompass and that external assistance cannot directly reach.

Alleviation of this poverty, the poverty of the poorest 40 per cent of the citizenry, is of immense urgency since the condition of these people is in fact far worse than national averages suggest. World Bank studies, for example, indicate that:

- In ten countries, with per capita incomes averaging $145, the poorest 40 per cent of the population receive a per capita income of only $50.

- In another ten countries with per capita incomes averaging $275, the poorest 40 per cent of the population receive a per capita income of only $80.

We are dealing here with problems difficult to grasp in their concrete, day-to-day realities. When we reflect that of the more than half a billion persons living on the Indian subcontinent, some 200 million subsist on incomes that average less than $40 a year, how are we to comprehend what that really implies? The estimate is that, if India were to depend exclusively on the growth of national income to solve its massive nutrition problems, it would require more than thirty years before the poorest third of the country could afford an adequate diet.

When we reflect that of the two billion persons living in our developing member countries, nearly two-thirds, or some 1.3 billion, are members of farm families, and that of these there are some 900 million whose annual incomes average less than $100, what frame of reference are we to call on to make that fact meaningful?

To many in the affluent world, to be a farmer suggests a life of dignity and decency, free of the irritation and pollution of modern existence, a life close to nature and rich in satisfactions. That may be what life on the land ought to be, but, for hundreds of millions of these subsistence farmers, life is neither satisfying nor decent. Hunger and malnutrition menace their families. Illiteracy forecloses their futures. Disease and death visit their villages too often, stay too long, and return too soon.

Their nation may be developing, but their lives are not. The miracle of the Green Revolution may have arrived, but, for the most part, the poor farmer has not been able to participate in it. He simply cannot afford to pay for the irrigation, the pesticide, the fertilizer, or perhaps even for the land itself, on which his title may be vulnerable and his tenancy uncertain. His nation may have doubled or tripled its educational budget, and in the capital city there may be an impressive university. But for 300 million children of poor farmers like himself there are still no schools—and for hundreds of millions of others if there is a school, no qualified teacher—and if a qualified teacher, no adequate books.

His nation may be improving its communications, and jet aircraft may be landing at its international airport in increasing numbers. But for the poor farmer who has seldom seen an airplane, and never an airport, what communications really means—and what he all too often does not have—is a simple all-weather road that would allow him to get his meager harvest to market when the time is right and the prices are good.

What these men want are jobs for their survival, food for their families, and a future for their children. They want the simple satisfaction of working toward something better—an end to misery and a beginning of hope.

We are not talking here about a few maladjusted discontents. We are talking about hundreds of millions of desperately poor people throughout the whole of the developing world. We are talking about 40 per cent of entire populations. Development is simply not reaching them in any decisive degree. Their countries are growing in gross economic terms, but their individual lives are stagnating in human terms.

Why is this the case? Why should economic growth at 5 per cent or 6 per cent leave so many untouched in their poverty? Is economic growth itself a delusion leading inevitably to disaster? No. Economic growth is a necessary condition of the broad development of any poor country, but it is far from a sufficient condition. Without a climate of growth, the domestic savings and export earnings crucial for internal investment simply cannot be mobilized. That is obvious enough. What is less obvious is that economic growth in a poor country, in its early stages, is likely to penalize the poorest segment of the society relative to the more affluent sectors unless specific action is taken to prevent such an effect.

This is particularly true of those subsistence agrarian economies in which economic growth began with a narrow but intense exploitation of rich natural resources. The historical experience of these situations is that unless the government takes steps to broaden the base of development by rapid reinvestment of the export revenues from such resources, the income share of the poorest 60 per cent of the population decreases and the income share of the richest 5 per cent increases.

Even the small middle-income group in such societies—
that approximate 20 per cent of the population whose
average share of the national income clusters near the median
point—even this incipient middle class receives a declining
share of the national income when growth is sudden and too
confined to enclave types of activity.

As development in a poor country broadens its base, the
middle-income group begins to benefit. This group prospers
largely as a function of its education and employment opportunities. But the 30 to 40 per cent of the total population,
who range from the poor to the very poor, continue to
receive a disproportionately small and frequently declining
share of national income. Typically, it is these poorest 40
per cent who are most vulnerable to the economic hardships
associated with high birth rates, poor educational opportunities, mounting inflation, the difficulty of obtaining credit for
family farming or small-scale local enterprises, and the migration from a stagnant countryside to a jobless urban slum.

If we are to solve this problem, we should begin by analyz-
ing the policy options that are generally proposed. They
present clearly conflicting schools of thought.

One view is that governments in developing countries
should make rapid economic growth the first objective. Income redistribution and increased employment can be
achieved later through fiscal and institutional changes.

Others argue that the growing pressures of poverty are
so overwhelming that their widespread relief should be the
central objective of development strategy, even if that entails
major sacrifice in the pace of over-all growth.

It would be comforting, of course, to continue to believe
that there is no conflict between rapid over-all growth and
comparable improvement in the incomes of the poor. Un-
fortunately, in the real world in which we live, the evidence
suggests that there is. There is a natural tendency for growth

to be concentrated in the modern sectors of the economy with little current benefit to the lowest income groups. What data there are, while admittedly incomplete, indicate that this pattern of growth has developed in many countries.

But, if few dispute the fact that there exists some conflict between maximization of growth and the rapid reduction of poverty, many argue that in the long term the conflict is irrelevant, since, given sufficient time, it can be resolved. In the long term, rapid growth will increase productivity and furnish the resources that can be redistributed to those who cannot yet be accommodated in the high-productivity, high-wage, modern sector.

The same view holds that even in the shorter term—a decade, say—it is possible at least to reduce the conflict between rapid growth and more equitable income for the poor by shaping an economy that provides the proper incentives, prices labor and capital correctly, strengthens the fiscal system, and emphasizes the right adaptive technologies.

Although this argument is correct as far as it goes, it doesn't go far enough. A decade may be the short term for a development planner, but a decade is the long term for a subsistence tenant farmer whose children are likely to die before the age of five, whose diet is already so inadequate that he cannot stave off chronic ill health, whose illiteracy limits his future ability to learn new skills, and whose perpetual indebtedness to the moneylender and dependence on the landowner leave him neither options nor hope.

On the other hand, one must recognize that if a government were to initiate policies to increase the income growth of the lowest 40 per cent of the population—to ensure that, at a minimum, their share of the nation's over-all economic growth does not decline as it has in the past—there are legitimate questions as to what the impact of such policies would be on the rate of over-all national growth. Would it seriously hamper it? Would it prevent it altogether? What precisely would happen?

There are at least three possible consequences of economic policies directed to more equitable income distribution that are thought to hamper growth. They are: reduced entrepreneurial incentives, lower savings rates, and the choice of obsolete technology.

Entrepreneurial incentives. It is often suggested that wide disparities in income are necessary in order to provide entrepreneurial incentives. Without arguing whether such incentives are important stimuli to productivity, one can question the amount of incentive that is required to motivate the desired degree of effort. In a study of the income disparities of 39 developing countries, in which the income of the wealthiest 5 per cent of the population is measured as a multiple of the bottom 40 per cent, there is a wide range of differences among countries. In 8 of the 39 countries the per capita income of the top 5 per cent is more than 30 times greater than that of the lowest 40 per cent. In 16 countries the ratio is less than 15 to 1. (In the United States, the ratio is 5 to 1.)

The significant point is that when one compares these two sets of countries on the basis of their per capita growth performance during the 1960's, there is no discernible relationship between the size of the incentives and the rapidity of growth. The average rate of growth of the group of countries with the greatest disparities was not significantly different from the group with the least. This indicates that there may well be substantial scope in the developing countries for moderating the highly skewed disparities in income without crippling the incentives to greater productivity.

Savings rates. Similarly, flexibility in the relationship between income distribution and the volume of savings available for socially productive investment may, in fact, be far greater than is generally assumed. While it is true that higher incomes permit a higher rate of savings, the real question is what becomes of those savings. If they are used for production of luxury goods to meet a demand pattern distorted by a skewed income distribution, it is questionable whether the high savings rate is, in fact, promoting any crucial national interest. If, on the other hand, a more equitable distribution of income results in a somewhat lower gross rate of savings but more investment in the production of essential commodities, the lower rate of growth in national income may be accompanied by an increase in the incomes of the bulk of the population.

Choice of technology. Finally, there is the question of the choice of technology. It is often asserted that rapid economic growth demands adoption of technologies that, by their very nature, penalize employment and perpetuate poverty. The argument is that unless the modern sector is so equipped, its inefficiencies will restrict the country's capacity to export and will perpetuate a costly dependence on imports for even the most basic requirements.

Here again, the argument is oversimplified. The issue is not so much modern technology versus traditional technology as efficient technology versus inefficient technology, and the essential question is how ought one to measure that efficiency. Efficiency is a relative term. A technology is efficient or inefficient relative to the resources one has available. In a labor-scarce, affluent, developed economy, the most efficient technology is capital-intensive and highly automated. It produces at the lowest cost per unit in terms of the scarce resource—labor.

But in a developing economy, where labor is abundant, and sophisticated skills are scarce, it is clearly inefficient to emulate technologies which lead to high costs per unit measured in terms of the scarce resource—capital. And yet that is the result when, in the rush to industrialize, developing countries subsidize capital by creating a structure in which foreign exchange is undervalued, credit is underpriced, and tax incentives misdirected.

If government policy were directed toward promoting a price structure which reflected the scarcity values of labor and capital more realistically, the technological choice would be different. The result would be greater employment, broader income distribution, and more competitive patterns of production of precisely those labor-intensive goods which labor-scarce affluent countries need but cannot themselves produce inexpensively.

What, then, are we to conclude from this analysis?

The answer is that while we obviously do not know as much as we want to know about the relationship of more equitable income distribution to over-all economic growth, we know enough to conclude that:

- It is possible to design policies with the explicit goal of improving the conditions of life of the poorest 40 per cent of the populations in the developing countries—and that this can be done without unacceptable penalties to the concomitant goal of national growth.

- Without specific emphasis on such programs, there will not be significant progress in reducing poverty within acceptable time periods.

We know, in effect, that there is no rational alternative to moving toward policies of greater social equity.

When the highly privileged are few and the desperately poor are many—and when the gap between them is worsening rather than improving—it is only a question of time before a decisive choice must be made between the political costs of reform and the political risks of rebellion. "Too little too late" is history's most universal epitaph for political regimes that have lost their mandate to the demands of landless, jobless, disenfranchised, and desperate men. That is why policies specifically designed to reduce the deprivation among the poorest 40 per cent in developing countries are prescriptions not only of principle but of prudence. Social justice is not merely a moral imperative. It is a political imperative as well.

What, then, can be done to attack the problem of massive poverty within the developing world?

The first and obvious step is the political resolve to make the effort. It is clear that in the end each country must make its own decision as to how and when to deal with its internal inequities. The problems of poverty are rooted deeply in the institutional frameworks, particularly in the distribution of economic and political power within the system. Outside agencies can assist but cannot solve such problems. Governments alone are responsible for essential domestic reform, and there is no way they can escape that responsibility. To postpone reform on the grounds of political expediency is to invite political extremism. To remain indifferent to social frustration is to foster its growth.

Political will, then, is the first requisite.

Public understanding is the second. All of us need a clearer perception of the problem. We need both more and better quantitative data on past and current trends in employment and in income distribution. And we need them urgently. I propose that the developing countries address this task of gathering income data and that as a practical matter they set a target date for a greatly expanded program of censuses, sample surveys, and specific studies. The international agencies—the World Bank included—can assist technically and financially and provide a multilateral forum for this effort.

Third, all of us need to identify concrete policies and actions that will reduce the skewness of the income distribution. Admittedly, we are on the frontier of a new field of knowledge here, and we have far more questions than we have answers. But the urgency of the situation is such that we simply cannot wait until all the answers are in. We must begin now with what we know now. And we clearly know enough to at least make a beginning. If we make mistakes, we will have to learn from them. The greatest mistake of all would be for the international development community to sit back and continue to do in the future what it has done in the past— ignore the problem. It is time for new approaches.

What ought they to be? Let me suggest a few of the most important:

• The first step should be to establish specific targets, within the development plans of individual countries, for income growth among the poorest 40 per cent of the population. I suggest that our goal should be to increase the income of the poorest sections of society in the short run (in five years) at least as fast as the national average. In the longer run (ten years) the goal should be to increase this growth significantly faster than the national average.

• Given the intimate link between poverty and massive unemployment, unemployment and underemployment must be attacked head-on. With 20 per cent or more of entire populations already jobless or virtually idle, and with the population explosion pouring a growing stream of new entrants into the labor pool each year, unless policies and programs are devised to absorb surplus labor into productive jobs, little can be done to improve the lot of the desperately poor. Job creation must therefore become a direct objective in itself. It will be necessary to organize rural and urban public works —the building of market roads, construction of low-cost simple housing, reforestation programs, expansion of irrigation and drainage facilities, highway maintenance, and similar low-

skill, labor-intensive, and economically useful projects. The
Bank will assist in financing such projects.

• Institutional reforms to redistribute economic power are
critically required in many developing countries—land reform, corporate reform, tax reform, credit and banking
reform, and many others. Continuation of the existing land
tenure patterns, tax laws, and banking regulations will simply
ensure that the present distribution of assets and income will
be perpetuated. The Bank will support reforms in these
areas with technical and financial assistance.

• Shifts in the patterns of public expenditure represent one
of the most effective techniques a government possesses to
improve the conditions of the poor. Too often these expenditures—on health, on transport, on water supply, on
education, and on many other sectors—end by benefiting the
already privileged far more than the mass of the disadvantaged. This is strikingly illustrated in the access to public
services. School enrollment ratios and the quality of education, for instance, are almost uniformly higher in the higher
income groups. In a sample of twenty developing countries,
the allocation of scarce foreign exchange was ten times greater
for the importation of private cars than for public buses.
This, in part, is because these services are more concentrated
in the urban areas and better neighborhoods. But it is also
a function of the greater participation of the highly privileged
in the political process. Governments can best begin to shift
public expenditure toward those who need it the most by
initiating surveys on the effects of their current patterns of
disbursement. Where do the funds really go? Who benefits
the most? The Bank will assist in such surveys and, based on
them, will help design programs, to be financed by it and
others, that will improve the distribution of public services.

• Finally, policies should be undertaken to eliminate distortions in the prices of land, labor, and capital. To underprice capital for the wealthy and make credit expensive for the poor; to allow liberal access to scarce resources for the privileged, and price them out of reach of the deprived; to provide subsidies for the powerful, and deny them to the powerless —these are wholly self-defeating approaches to development. Such policies lead a nation inevitably toward economic imbalance and social instability.

These, then, are the general measures that all of us in the international development community should undertake with all the urgency at our command. We in the World Bank can assist our developing member countries in this effort, and we fully intend to do so.

Epilogue

In my first speech to the Governors of the World Bank I put forward a Five-Year Program. In my fifth speech to the Governors, in September, 1972, I recalled what we set out to accomplish:

Our analysis of the over-all requirements for economic progress in our developing member countries convinced us that we should greatly broaden and expand the World Bank's operations both in scope and in size.

We proposed as our over-all lending objective a doubling of the World Bank's operations in the fiscal period 1969–73, as compared with the period 1964–68. Were we to achieve this goal, it would mean that during the five years 1969–73 the volume of lending would approach the total amount lent during the previous twenty-three years of the Bank's operations.

I can report now that we will not only meet that goal but will surpass it.

But it was not principally the size of our operations that concerned us when we launched the Five-Year Program. We did not merely want to do more. We wanted to do more of what would contribute most to development. Thus, within the over-all lending program, we were resolved to shift our emphasis both into different sectors and into different geographical areas.

What does that mean in practice?

• In a developing world in which hunger is chronic, it means intensifying our efforts in agriculture. We have quadrupled our operations in that sector.

• In a developing world darkened by functional illiteracy, it means expanding our efforts in education. We have tripled our operations in that sector.

• In a developing world caught up in the threat of unmanageable population pressures, it means facing up to that complex and controversial problem. We have established a Population Projects Department, and we have launched important initiatives in that sector.

In our previous meetings, I have stressed the damaging effect of runaway population growth on a developing economy. I have pointed out the strains this creates both at the family and the national level for any country struggling to improve the quality of life for its people.

Overly rapid population growth simply erodes and dissipates development gains in every sector. Savings evaporate, scarcities multiply, and resources are stretched so thin that in the end they cannot cover the most essential needs.

While the population problem is clearly one which cannot

be solved within the confines of a five-year plan, or a development decade—or indeed even during what is left of our century—it is by its very nature a problem that can grow only worse with procrastination and delay. That is why we believe the entire international community must assign it the highest priority.

The Bank's initial work in the population field consisted of sector missions to a dozen different countries and projects deliberately initiated in smaller member countries in order to provide us with working experience on a scale commensurate with our new capabilities.

But in the early summer of 1972 we approved far-reaching projects in two of our largest member nations: India and Indonesia.

The project in India, a joint effort with the Government of Sweden, will develop what promises to be the most advanced systems approach to the population problem in any developing country. It will provide the essential information and analysis required to shape the over-all massive effort India is making to reduce its current population growth.

Both the size of India's problem and the magnitude of its effort to solve it can be grasped in the statistics. The nation's total population now stands at over half a billion. It is growing by an additional million each month. The government has set up an organization of 80,000 persons to administer a family-planning program to serve 100 million couples. The Bank project is designed to help support that program with the experimentation and the systems analyses required to make it effective.

Like India, Indonesia is serious in its determination to provide its people with effective family-planning assistance. With a population of more than 120 million, currently growing at an annual rate of 2.5 per cent, it ranks fifth among the world's most heavily populated countries. Some two-thirds of its people live in Java and Bali, where the average density is nearly 1,600 persons per square mile.

With the participation of the United Nations Fund for Population Activities, the World Health Organization, Unesco, and UNICEF, the Bank project provides $13 million for a greatly expanded family-planning program. In addition to the construction of 300 health centers and the provision of the required vehicles and equipment, the project will help finance the training of several thousand field workers, the preparation of public school curricula, and a program of research and evaluation.

Should the over-all objectives of the project be reached—and both the Indonesian Government and we are confident that they can—Indonesia's population by the end of the century, even though it will be twice as large as it is today, will be 50 million less than it would otherwise be.

What all this demonstrates is that our Five-Year Program has shifted the Bank's emphasis toward those sectors which under today's conditions require intensified effort: agriculture, education, and population. As I have indicated, our shifts in emphasis have been geographical as well as sectoral. In Africa, we expect to more than treble our lending over the previous five-year period. For our poorest member countries—those whose per capita incomes average less than $100—we will quadruple our lending.

To achieve these goals has, of course, required a substantial strengthening of the World Bank both organizationally and financially. The professional staff, for example, by the end of the five-year period will have increased by 125 per cent.

Recruitment of highly qualified staff, representing the broadest possible geographical experience, has been facilitated by a worldwide interest in the work of the Bank. In the past year, more than 2,400 candidates, from 98 countries, applied for 52 available openings in our Young Professionals Program.

Doubling the volume of our lending operations has meant, of course, that we had greatly to expand our borrowing capacity. This in turn depends on governments granting us access to their countries' capital markets. Despite recurrent and unsettling readjustments in the international monetary system, they have continued to do so.

Not only have we continued to borrow in our more traditional markets but we have entered new markets as well and have utilized new borrowing instruments and new channels of distribution. Net borrowing for the five-year period will approximate three and three-quarter times that of the earlier period and liquid reserves will increase by about 125 per cent.

Neither the expansion of operations nor the shift into less traditional sectors of lending has adversely affected net income. On the contrary, total net income during the five-year period will be approximately 30 per cent higher than that of the previous period, and this despite a significant increase in the subsidy to the developing countries implicit in the Bank's lending rate.

Organizationally, then, and financially, the World Bank will complete the first Five-Year Program in a position of strength. But while encouragement over the Bank's operations is one thing, complacency with the state of development is quite another. There is little danger of confusing the two if we will recall the discussion in the previous chapters of the pressing requirement that exists today for additional development assistance. In summary I have pointed out:

● In its strategy for the Second Development Decade, the United Nations set as a target that the average annual rate of growth in gross national product for the developing countries should be at least 6 per cent. To make that possible, the developed countries were to increase their concessionary aid (Official Development Assistance, or ODA) to .7 per cent of their GNP's by 1975.

• It is now clear that the objective of .7 per cent will not be reached. There seems little likelihood that during the first half of the decade ODA will exceed .37 per cent of GNP— only half of the Second Development Decade target. That is regrettable in the extreme, but we must be realistic. And realism dictates that we try to assess the effects of this massive shortfall in concessionary aid.

• The first, and least tolerable, of the effects is that the poorer of our member countries—those with per capita GNP's of less than $200—will be penalized the most. Their needs for Official Development Assistance are the greatest, and their chances for finding feasible alternatives are the least. What is more, these countries collectively contain 1.1 billion people, 64 per cent of the aggregate population of our entire developing country membership. They are the very countries which have suffered the greatest burdens of poverty during the past decade. Their GNP's grew annually at an average of only 4.1 per cent, and their per capita incomes at a minuscule 1.7 per cent.

• With the ODA objective only half achieved, these poorer nations have almost no hope of attaining the 6 per cent growth target. That will condemn them to so slow an economic advance over the decade that hundreds of millions of individuals within these countries will be able to detect virtually no improvement whatever in their desperately low standards of living. Their per capita incomes will rise by no more than $2.00 a year.

• Projected to the end of the century—only a generation away —this means the people of the developed countries will be enjoying per capita incomes, in 1972 prices, of over $8,000 a year, while these masses of the poor (who by that time will total over 2.25 billion) will on average receive less than $200 per capita, and some 800 million of these will receive less than $100.

The deficit in development assistance will penalize the poorest countries the most. But even for those developing countries which are somewhat better off, a deficiency in ODA will cause serious economic and financial problems.

Publicly guaranteed debt in the developing world currently stands at about $80 billion, with annual debt service of approximately $7 billion. Debt service payments rose by 18 per cent in 1970 and by 20 per cent in 1971, representing twice the average rate of increase over the 1960's and reflecting a hardening of the terms of debts, while the proportion of concessionary aid in the total flow of external assistance to developing countries declined.

Given the shortfall in ODA and the growing debt problem, it seems clear that the World Bank should try to continue to expand its operations. If we were to fail to make this effort, our developing member countries would be driven to an even greater dependence on higher-cost, shorter-maturity sources of external capital with the inevitable exacerbation of their debt-servicing burdens. They would have little choice, for without a reasonable flow of external finance they simply cannot meet even minimal development requirements.

For the World Bank to relax in its resolve to do everything it feasibly can to assist in this situation would be to shirk our central responsibility, which is to recommend those policies, provide that technical assistance, and help finance those projects that will most effectively support our developing member countries' own struggle to advance the welfare of their people.

With careful planning and the support of the Governors of the Bank, we are convinced that the World Bank can obtain the necessary funds to continue to expand its operations during a Second Five-Year Program. And that is what we propose to do.

As an over-all goal, for the fiscal year period 1974–78, we propose to increase our financial commitments to our developing member countries by an average of 11 per cent a year and to shift an increasing percentage of these commitments to International Development Association credits.

If we can achieve this expanded level of operations—and I am confident that it is possible—it means that the World Bank will help finance and provide technical assistance for some $50 billion of capital improvements in our developing member countries during the period of the Second Five-Year Program.

Standing on the threshold of a new Five-Year Program at the Bank, I remain optimistic about the future of the world and the majority of its inhabitants, who live in developing countries. I remain an optimist because I have visited many of those countries and have seen with my own eyes how great an effort they are making to improve their own lot. I cannot believe that the affluent world will fail to play its small but crucial part in assisting the betterment of its neighbors. I am determined that the Bank shall play its full part as an active and skilled agency for the development of the people of the world.

Appendix: Financing the International Bank for Reconstruction and Development*

M ore than once I have sought to emphasize a point that my predecessors Eugene Black and George Woods made over and over again: The International Bank for Reconstruction and Development (IBRD) is not only a financial institution—it is a development agency. I accepted my present position with the World Bank because I believe that the development of the emerging world is one of the biggest and the most important tasks confronting mankind in this century.

* The source of this appendix is my address to the Bond Club of New York, 1969, explaining the financial structure of the IBRD. Statistics have been updated to 1972.

But, having said that, I must make equally clear that the IBRD is a development investment institution, not a philanthropic organization and not a social welfare agency. Our lending policy is founded on two basic principles: The project must be sound; and the borrower must be creditworthy. We simply will not make a loan unless both these criteria can be met—and met completely.

We insist that the investment project itself have a demonstrably high economic return and be directly related to the development of the country in which it is located. And we insist further that the economy of the borrowing nation be capable of repaying our loan and meeting the interest and other charges on schedule. These have been the IBRD's criteria from the very beginning. They are going to remain its criteria in the future.

With more than twenty-five years of accumulated experience, the IBRD's appraisal of the technological feasibility and the economic value of new investment projects is today more sound, more searching, and more sophisticated than it has ever been. As for the creditworthiness of our clients, I am fully aware that certain countries face mounting problems of debt management. Past burdens can tend to depress future ability to meet new obligations. We initiated, therefore, a special study of this problem to ensure that we lend only where there is a firm basis for repayment.

Our studies of creditworthiness are not just passive examinations of how a country is managing its economic affairs. They are increasingly designed to make specific suggestions on how policies and programs can be improved. Changes in economic policies—once accomplished—can work near miracles in improving the creditworthiness of a country. But although the IBRD will continue to lend only on the financial principles of sound projects and creditworthy clients, I am convinced that within the limits of those principles we can and should greatly expand our lending program if we are to fulfill our obligations to our member states. Let me explain why.

First, I want to emphasize that what I am discussing here is the IBRD arm of the World Bank—the International Bank for Reconstruction and Development. The IBRD is essentially a "hard lender." There are, of course, countries in desperate need of development capital that simply cannot qualify for "hard" loans. As far as the World Bank is concerned, their capital requirements must be met by our affiliate, the International Development Association, which obtains its funds from government appropriations of member countries.

But it is not the International Development Association that I am describing here. I am talking about the IBRD and therefore about our "hard-loan" operations, and the issues are these: Do the developing countries need more of these hard loans, and is the IBRD able to make them? Based on the most careful analysis, my colleagues and I are convinced the answer to both questions is yes.

If one looks around the globe today, it is obvious the world is characterized by an expanding economy. The industrially advanced nations are, of course, the leading edge of this surge of progess. But there are a number of developing nations as well—countries such as Malaysia and Mexico, for example—that are experiencing dramatic economic growth under the infusion of modern management, new technology, and development capital.

In the field of agriculture, we have the beginnings of a revolutionary breakthrough on our hands. The massive improvement in wheat and rice cultivation in Southeast Asia is momentous. It is no mere freak of good weather or lucky conditions. It is a carefully planned program of new seeds, intensive use of fertilizer, and modern soil and water management. The Green Revolution is not simply a grab bag of miscellaneous farm techniques. It is a complete and co-ordinated agricultural technology. If we can succeed in marrying this technology to new programs of agricultural credit and marketing, we can definitely arrest the spread of famine that threatens the world's exploding population.

But it is not in agriculture alone that economic opportunity is strong. Korea, for example, has recently achieved annual increases in industrial production of 24 per cent, and in industrial exports of 42 per cent. This is economic expansion at an extraordinary rate, and suggests that the modernization of Japan over a few decades may not have been an isolated phenomenon.

These nations, and many others like them, all require development capital—capital to expand the irrigation systems, capital to build the fertilizer plants, capital to construct the storage facilities, capital to turn the immense agricultural potential into a self-sustaining reality. And they require comparable capital to stimulate and bring to the take-off point their indigenous industrial production.

Capital requirements throughout the developing world have not diminished; they have expanded. The opportunities for high-return investment have mounted almost everywhere. As in the past, 85 per cent of the new capital required will come out of the savings of the developing countries themselves. But that 85 per cent will remain ineffectual without the other 15 per cent, which is the irreducible foreign-exchange component these countries must borrow from abroad.

The irony is that just at the very moment when the opportunities for productive investment of external capital are expanding, the flow of that capital as a percentage of GNP—particularly from the United States—has begun to shrink.

Why it is shrinking is a complicated story which we need not pursue here, beyond noting that there are two important assumptions at work here that are clearly erroneous. One is that the richer countries can no longer afford to supply capital abroad; and the second is that, even if they could afford it, it would be unwise, since the over-all record of developmental investment is a dismal picture of waste, incompetence, and failure.

These popular conceptions are simply not based on fact. But the more important point is this: How can we deal with a paradoxical situation in which significant opportunities for prudent investment in the developing world have increased, and yet in which the flow of investment funds has flagged rather than quickened?

The IBRD in the spring of 1968 initiated a series of studies to determine what could be done to resolve that paradox. When all the data had been sifted and thoroughly examined, the conclusion was compelling. Our studies demonstrated beyond any question that the demand of the developing countries for hard loans, on standards as high or even higher than in the past, would expand substantially.

Though one could not predict with absolute precision what the new investment opportunities would justify in total lending year by year when matched against the IBRD's lending criteria, the estimate was that it would warrant an increase, for a five-year period, of at least 100 per cent. It seemed reasonable that the Bank could and should embark on such a course—a lending program specifically designed to help countries improve their economic performance. Indeed, this is a program designed to improve the economic performance of the world as a whole.

The lending program is, of course, only one side of the coin. If we were to double our lending, we clearly had to borrow more. Further, we wanted to try to improve our liquidity. In the years prior to 1968, the IBRD's balances of cash and liquid resources had been reduced by approximately

$400 million from previous levels, because of the difficulties of borrowing in the world capital markets.

Was the five-year target of a 100 per cent increase in loans, plus the desired increase in liquidity, practical in terms of our bond sales? In broad terms, what we proposed to do was to substantially increase the IBRD's borrowings and increase its cash position considerably in order to support the projected lending program. The IBRD succeeded in meeting this goal. From April, 1968, through December, 1972, the Bank borrowed the equivalent of over $6 billion on a gross basis, and its liquid cash position increased from $1.4 billion to $3.4 billion, an increase of $2 billion from the 1968 levels. That did not seem to us then—nor does it seem to us now —an unrealistically large amount of borrowing on the world-wide capital market.

It is important to remember that one of the principal advantages of the IBRD is that it can raise money in any member country that opens its market to it and that provides fully convertible currency. This means that IBRD can spread its financing throughout a large number of nations. What we have done in recent years is to look for new sources of funds. We have found them, for example, in Kuwait, Lebanon, Libya, and Saudi Arabia.

In the late 1960's, we began to borrow substantial amounts of new resources in the Federal Republic of Germany. In fiscal years 1969 through 1972 we borrowed the equivalent of $952 million in the German public market through syndicates managed by our long-term underwriters (the Deutsche Bank); from the Westdeutsche Landesbank (a major clearinghouse for savings institutions); and from other quasi-public financial institutions. Further, the Deutsche Bundesbank has continued to be a main supplier of IBRD resources. It held the equivalent of over $700 million (exclusive of two-year bond holdings) of IBRD obligations as of June 30, 1972.

In the last two years a major provider of the IBRD's funds has been Japan. The IBRD has borrowed $834 million from the Bank of Japan since February, 1970, and on five occasions has borrowed an aggregate equivalent to $253 million in the Japanese public markets.

In the last five years we have also borrowed substantial resources from over sixty Central Banks through our two-year U.S. dollar bond issues, of which $770.8 million are now outstanding.

In addition, the IBRD has been able to obtain new resources from commercial banks throughout the world, which have provided us with relatively long-term capital through IBRD loans and private placements.

In virtually every country the amounts and frequency of our issues have increased as the IBRD has diversified its methods and places of borrowing. In two fiscal years 1971 and 1972 we borrowed more than in any similar previous period of the IBRD's history, with gross borrowings equivalent to $3.1 billion. In those years 74 per cent of our gross borrowing was outside of the U.S. market.

It should not be surprising that our securities enjoy so high a rating. The combination of assets and guarantees that provides their intrinsic strength is wholly unique. It consists of:

- A portfolio of loans for projects that bring high economic returns to the borrower—returns that run as high as 90 per cent and average well over 10 per cent per year.

- A guarantee of 100 per cent repayment of each loan by the government of the country in which the project is located.

- Cash and liquid security balances, in fully convertible currencies, equal to about 46 per cent of the outstanding IBRD debt.

- Paid-in capital and retained earnings amounting to 61 per cent of our debt.

- All this, plus uncalled capital subscriptions backing the IBRD securities and equal to some 340 per cent of the amount of debt outstanding.

No other bond in the world offers that kind of security. And it is precisely because of the strength of that security—and our stated determination to maintain that strength—that we have been able to place our recent bond issues at favorable rates. Typically, IBRD bonds are sold in capital markets throughout Europe and the Far East at yields that approximate yields on obligations of governments in such markets.

In essence, IBRD bonds are backed by the strongest industrial nations on earth. And yet, we have always proceeded as if this outside protection of our bonds did not in fact exist. We have sought so to conduct our business that the IBRD need never call on that security—and we have succeeded. In my view, the most persuasive guarantee of our bonds is the prudent day-to-day operation of the IBRD by its experienced and expert staff. I am determined to make certain that this guarantee is the only one we will ever have to exercise.

In fiscal years 1969–73, profits will average approximately $192 million, compared to average annual profits during the 1964–68 period of $145 million.

Today a typical twenty-five-year IBRD loan, which carries an interest rate of 7.25 per cent, contains a grant element of approximately 20 per cent of the face value of the loan. The combination of concessionary interest rates to our borrowers and operating profits to our stockholders is made possible by our high ratio of interest-free capital and accumulated savings ($4.3 billion) to funded debt (approximately $7 billion as of June 30, 1972). At that time, the average cost to the IBRD for all its funds—that is, its total funded debt plus its paid-in capital and retained earnings—was only 4 per cent. Essentially, it is the difference between this 4 per cent and the IBRD's interest rate on outstanding loans (now 7.25 per cent on new loans) that enables us to cover all our administrative costs, grant reasonable concessions to our borrowers, and continue to earn substantial profits.

But, though profits have been good, there is a far more fundamental basis for our reputation, and that, of course, is the choice and supervision of our overseas investments. Outsiders have been immensely impressed by the professional competence with which our staff analyzes both the specific project and the economy of the borrowing country before a loan is made—and by the careful scrutiny and supervision of the project after the loan is made.

Such deep involvement in the domestic economies of independent (often newly independent) countries is possible only because the borrowing nation understands and appreciates our genuine dedication to its development. They see us for what we in fact are—an international agency specializing in development, with no political axe to grind. The security of our investment depends on our borrowers' development. Hence, their interests and ours coincide.

It is on these strict standards of appraisal and supervision that the reputation of the IBRD rests. These standards continue in full force during our expansion. That is possible because in twenty-seven years of experience we have learned a great deal about the techniques of realistic development planning and the successful supervision of projects in distant and often primitive surroundings.

This assimilated experience now allows us to cope efficiently with a much larger volume of work. As we expand, we must remain sufficiently flexible to change our emphasis as the needs of development itself change. It is no longer enough to invest in traditional infrastructure, such as power, transport, and communications. Both the needs and the opportunities in the developing world now point unmistakably to such fields as agriculture, education, and population planning. Let me make it clear that in these relatively new areas we will apply the same rigorous standards of both economic profitability of the project itself and creditworthiness of the country in question.

It is not as easy to quantify the economic benefits of a technical school as of a hydroelectric plant. Similarly, on the surface, it may appear that you have something more impressive and solid to show when you build a highway than when you simply sink a lot of tubewells, but the whole point is that a surface impression is not a sound economic analysis. A good irrigation system, for example, when combined with the use of new strains of seeds, can result in an economic return of 90 per cent a year. That is in fact an actual case that occurred in Pakistan.

When you reflect that the developing countries now require $4 billion a year of food imports, it is obvious that a broad expansion of their agricultural production can have an immensely beneficial effect on their balance of payments situation—and thus enhance their over-all creditworthiness.

The economists at the IBRD have been working on methods for quantifying the economic returns derived from social investment, such as education. Their conclusions demonstrate that the benefits vary enormously. A liberal arts college in a private underdeveloped area can be a dead loss, but a technical high school—in an expanding economy where the available capital is not matched by the requisite skilled manpower—can pay huge dividends. One such project in Latin America brought an annual return of 50 per cent. It is the IBRD's task to determine, in a given situation, precisely what

sort of education contributes most to solid economic growth
and to invest accordingly. We have not financed in the past,
and we will not finance in the future, any education project
that is not directly related to that economic growth.

In developing countries with excessive birth rates, loans in
the field of population planning have perhaps the highest
economic benefits of all. Unless the rampant rate of population growth is reasonably moderated in many of these nations,
not only will their developmental projects be finally overwhelmed, but their capability of repaying foreign loans will
be eroded within a decade or two.

Let me summarize IBRD's situation.

I have noted that we conduct our affairs as though the only
security behind our bonds were the technical and financial
soundness of the projects themselves in our loan portfolio.
But behind that assurance stands our very favorable ratio
of equity to debt. Our total debt as of June 30, 1972,
amounted to some $7 billion, compared to paid-in capital and
retained earnings of approximately $4.3 billion. Beyond this
lie two further assurances—two unique guarantees by the
governments of the world: first, that each loan is the primary
or guarantee obligation of the country in which the IBRD's
investment is made; second, that the total of all IBRD debt
is backed by the uncalled capital subscriptions of the member
governments—capital that can be used for no other purpose.

In the twenty-seven-year history of the IBRD, there have
been no losses on its loans. No government has failed to honor
its obligations. The Bank has not been a target for debt
repudiation as have bilateral aid agencies and private credit
corporations. The reason is obvious. Developing nations are
convinced that it is in their own best interest to maintain im-
peccable relations with the IBRD. This holds true even in
extreme situations, such as existed during the later years of the

Nkrumah regime in Ghana or in the period when the United Arab Republic defaulted on obligations to bilateral creditors. Neither of these governments defaulted on IBRD loans. As we expand our operations and become a more and more important source of development capital, the advantage to borrowing countries of continuing to meet their obligations to us will increase.

The final security behind our bonds is represented by the uncalled subscriptions to IBRD capital. These amount at present to $24.6 billion, more than 3.3 times the total of our funded debt as of December 31, 1972. That $24.6 billion includes a U.S. share of $6.3 billion and a Common Market, United Kingdom, Canadian, and Japanese share of $9.1 billion.

The guarantee represented by the uncalled subscriptions cannot be eroded. By the provisions of our charter, these uncalled subscriptions may not be drawn upon for loans or administrative expenses. They can be used solely as a protection for the obligations of the IBRD. Moreover, the uncalled subscriptions are expressed in U.S. dollars of the weight and fineness in effect on July 1, 1944. Thus they are not subject to deterioration as a result of changes in the value of currencies.

Similarly, because the loans of the IBRD, made out of borrowed funds, are disbursed and repaid in the same currencies, the IBRD faces no devaluation risks on its borrowed funds: Its obligations to its creditors are matched by the repayments due from the borrowers.

It is, then, no exaggeration to say that the IBRD is an entirely unique financial institution.

It is unique in its security and strength.

And it is unique in its purpose and program.

The IBRD was founded in 1944 to help reconstruct and

develop a smashed, war-ravaged world. In the years since then it has been increasingly involved in assisting the developing world. And there the task is changing. I have described above our response to that change. It is the response of a vigorous and expanding organization—strong and secure in its financial base, prudent and precise in its decisions, and realistic in its goals.

Sources

The basic sources for each chapter are addresses delivered by Robert S. McNamara on the following occasions at the indicated places and times.

CHAPTER 1

Annual Meeting of the Board of Governors of the World Bank, Washington, D.C., September 30, 1968.

CHAPTER 2

University of Notre Dame, Notre Dame, Indiana, May 1, 1969.

CHAPTER 3

Annual Meetings of the Board of Governors of the World Bank, Copenhagen, September 21, 1970, and Washington, D.C., September 27, 1971.

Columbia University Conference on International Economic Development, New York City, February 20, 1970.

CHAPTER 4

United Nations Conference on Trade and Development, Santiago, April 14, 1972.

Annual Meeting of the Board of Governors of the World Bank, Washington, D.C., September 27, 1971.

CHAPTER 5

United Nations Conference on the Human Environment, Stockholm, June 8, 1972.

Columbia University Conference on International Economic Development, New York City, February 20, 1970.

CHAPTER 6

United Nations Conference on Trade and Development, Santiago, April 14, 1972.

Annual Meeting of the Board of Governors of the World Bank, Washington, D.C., September 25, 1972.

EPILOGUE

Annual Meeting of the Board of Governors of the World Bank, Washington, D.C., September 25, 1972.

APPENDIX

The Bond Club of New York, New York City, May 14, 1969.